STAR TREK

DESIGNING THE FINAL FRONTIER

DAN CHAVKIN • BRIAN McGUIRE

STAR TREK
DESIGNING THE FINAL FRONTIER

How Midcentury Modernism Shaped Our View of the Future

weldonowen

CONTENTS

06 Foreword by Doug Drexler

INTRODUCTION
08

ON THE BRIDGE
14

SEASON ONE
24

26 The Cage

30 The Corbomite Maneuver

34 The Man Trap

38 The Conscience of the King

44 Court Martial

48 A Taste of Armageddon

56 Operation -- Annihilate!

FUTURISTIC ARCHITECTURE
60

SEASON TWO
76

78 Metamorphosis

84 The Trouble with Tribbles

88 Assignment: Earth

96 SET DECORATION, PROPS, AND FASHION

116 SEASON THREE

118 The *Enterprise* Incident

122 For the World Is Hollow and I Have Touched the Sky

126 The Cloud Minders

130 BRUTALISM

144 MIDCENTURY ADVERTISING

152 CATALOG OF OBJECTS

162 Index

166 Credits

168 Acknowledgments

MIDCENTURY MODERN DESIGN, THE FORMS OF THINGS UNKNOWN, AND TECHNOLOGY UNCHAINED

I'm a sort of interstellar Billy Pilgrim. I, too, am unstuck in time, but I am unstuck in reality as well. I spring from reality to reality, universe to universe, starship to starship. At this point, it's pretty obvious that I am fated to this, that it defines me, and that it's not even a choice. It's written in my DNA.

It's Groundhog Day, except every time I wake up, I'm standing on the deck of a different starship, and I belong there. It is my expertise, my solar system, my planet, my country. The thrill is indescribable when I am in the presence of incredible science-fiction, space-oriented, set design. My knees buckle, my head swims, and blood rushes to my head. It's a form of wonderful derangement, like that of a salmon swimming upstream. Yes, I MUST do this. It wants me. I belong to it. I'm possessed.

I owe my career to the original *Star Trek*. It was my childhood love of the show that led me to become a film maker. Since *Star Trek's* premiere in 1966, I've won both American and British Academy Awards, been nominated for eight prime time Emmys (winning twice!), and taken home a Saturn Award, a Visual Effects Society Award, and a Peabody. I've worked with such directors as Warren Beatty, Mike Nichols, Richard Fleischer, Michael Cimino, and Michael Mann. Thank you, Gene Roddenberry, and Matt Jefferies.

As an illustrator, graphic designer, makeup artist, and visual effects artist, I've worked in more positions on Star Trek than anyone in the franchise's fifty-plus year history, contributing to *Star Trek: The Next Generation, Star Trek: Deep Space Nine, Star Trek: Voyager, Star Trek: Enterprise, Star Trek: Picard*, and four *Star Trek* motion pictures. I also claim the rare distinction of having designed two starships *Enterprise*.

Hollywood production design distills who we are as a culture, defines who we are to become in the distant future, and where we have been in the far-flung past. It gives shape and form to our dreams and aspirations. It shows us where we have been, and where we are going. It molds light and shadow, translating into emotions, and feelings, not just for the audience, but the director, the camera, and the actors in the play.

There is an old saying: If it isn't on the page, it isn't on the stage. Actor-Director John Cassavetes famously said if this were true, there would be no reason to make the movie. Midcentury Modern was never on the page, and as much as we enshrine the scribes who give depth and breadth to our cinematic fantasies, there is still no writer who could have written an aesthetic like Midcentury Modern.

Star Trek creator Gene Roddenberry defined the *Star Trek* design ethic as "Technology Unchained," where form does not necessarily always follow function, and that it is also driven by emotion, beauty, and the distinctly human predilection for bending the rules. This is the very definition of Midcentury Modern design. Original *Star Trek* production designer Matt Jefferies was smart. He knew this, and he recognized the intrinsic futurism, boldness, and courageousness embodied by the mid century design aesthetic.

The *Star Trek* design foundation can trace its roots back to the 1964-65 New York World's Fair, and it was a major influence on Jefferies. The event was a nexus of Midcentury Modern sci-fi extrapolation, influencing the look of science fiction films, and particularly *Star Trek*, to the present day. As a kid on the loose at the fair, I helped myself to all the printed material that I could carry. Three decades later, some of it ended up on the walls of the Trek art department as a source of inspiration.

Long before there was the internet, there were World's Fairs. That's how new ideas were introduced. Affluent American corporations opened their dream labs to a wide-eyed public, in person. It was only twenty years after World War II, and American industry was booming. The 1964-65 New York World's Fair was the largest international exhibition ever built in the United States, and it was all about THE FUTURE. Never before, and never again, would there be such an amazing conglomeration of Midcen-tury Modern futurism in one place. Matt Jefferies absorbed it all with intense fascination. Indeed, the New York World's Fair was the birthplace of the *Star Trek* design ethic. Pavilions for Ford (Welton Becket), General Motors (The GM styling staff headed by the legendary Bill Mitchell), New York State (Phillip Johnson), and Bell Systems (Harrison & Abramovitz) left an indelible mark on Matt, *Star Trek*, and me, too.

As science officer Spock observed, time could be perceived as a river, with eddies and backwashes. Someone else was washed up onto that World's Fair shore, and our paths undoubt-edly crossed at the jetting waters of the iconic Unisphere, or trekked side by side along the undulating Kodak Moon Deck, or stood in line at Ford's Magic Skyway. My fellow time traveler was Walter "Matt" Jefferies: aviator, illustrator, art director. He would become one of the most important artistic influences in my life. Forty years later, Matt would tell Mike Okuda and me what an impression the Fair had made on him. When he returned home from the exposition, there was a message waiting, ". . . from a guy named Roddenberry."

There is a culinary term, *amuse bouche*, which translates to "entertain the mouth," and then there is *amuse l'oeil*, which means "entertain the eye." When you entertain the eye, you tap into a supernaturally visceral and innate knowledge, rooted in emotion, style, imagination, and something seemingly indistinguishable from magic. Midcentury Modern.

—DOUG DREXLER, *NORTH HOLLYWOOD*

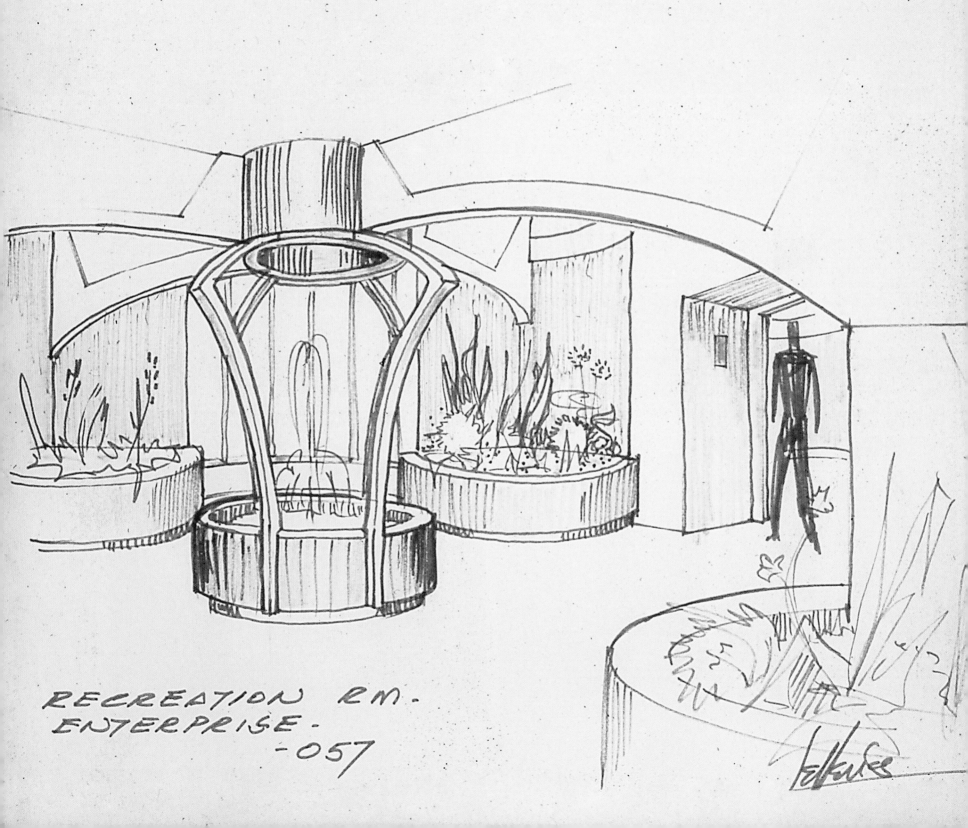

RECREATION RM.
ENTERPRISE.
-057

INTRODUCTION

LEFT Matt Jefferies' sketches shaped the overall look of *Star Trek* by channeling Midcentury Modernism. Pictured is a set design for an *Enterprise* recreation room never realized for Season Three's episode "Elaan of Troyius."

THE ORIGIN

My journey into the *Star Trek* universe began rather randomly. As I sought out a new television program to binge-watch, I turned to *Star Trek*—the show that will always have an extremely important place in the pantheon of science fiction and of American TV programming. So, being fully aware of its impact on popular culture, I was excited to experience, for the very first time, that which so many millions of people around the world have appreciated since its inception in 1966. And so began the journey.

To my great surprise, it was very shortly into the first season that I spotted, during the episode "The Man Trap," a piece of midcentury modern design—an Architectural Pottery planter by designer John Follis. It was framed in the doorway to the *Enterprise*'s botany section between the two characters in the foreground: Lieutenant Uhura and the salt vampire. Immediately, my curiosity was piqued even more so than by the ominous conflict unfolding in the episode. I thought it intriguing that a piece of notable pottery would appear not just on *Star Trek*, but specifically on the ship itself. I say "notable" because of my years of studying midcentury modern furniture and design. My next bit of spotting occurred during the beloved episode "The Corbomite Maneuver," also from the first season, in which the impish alien Balok uses another piece from Architectural Pottery as the control console of his spaceship, the *Fesarius*. Henceforth, I devoted myself to the task of documenting anything on the program identifiable from the midcentury modern genre.

In short, I conceived the idea for this book not as a devoted Trek fan, but rather as a midcentury modern enthusiast. As I began to watch more episodes of the show, little did I know that the three seasons of *Star Trek* would be host to so many examples of important midcentury modern design, placed thoughtfully and carefully by the art director and set decorators.

Finally, after having viewed all three seasons of *Star Trek*, I had amassed a catalog of midcentury modern furniture, art, and design appearing throughout the show. Thus, the concept for the book was born!

My research for the book included seeking out one of the few surviving set decorators of the show, John M. Dwyer. I thought it very useful to contact one of the behind-the-scenes principals, whose contribution to the show could support and enhance the book concept—a survey of midcentury modern design as seen on *Star Trek*. Most serendipitously, I was able to locate Dwyer, whose residence was close to mine and who ultimately agreed to an interview.

Upon meeting Dwyer, I was immediately charmed by a man whose manner was gentle and warm. I brought a selection of stills from the show I had made to spark his recollection. At first,

I asked him cursory questions about his background. "I'm a fourth-generation prop man," he said emphatically. "My father and brother were prop men. My father at one time worked for D.W. Griffith" (the legendary silent film director of *The Ten Commandments* and other early epic films)." Dwyer intimated that he had prepared for motion pictures his whole life. His father got him into the union so that he, too, could work as a prop man.

He told me that he joined *Star Trek* during the second season, performing the set decoration for "The Trouble with Tribbles." "We were given $500 dollars plus labor," he said, for pulling props for each episode. I then pressed him as to how he knew which type of props or pieces of furniture to use for the show. Quite simply, he said that he just knew what was appropriate for the episode. I asked him if he had been aware of the source of the chairs that appear in the bar fight scene in "Tribbles" designer Paul McCobb's Origami

LEFT The Platner Collection of furniture was introduced by Knoll Inc. in 1966, and early the next year made an appearance in Season One's "A Taste of Armageddon." RIGHT Vintage advertisement for Paul McCobb's Origami chairs, which made an appearance in Season Two's "The Trouble with Tribbles."

chairs) and he replied, "I wasn't too familiar with designers except for, say, Eames [the famous American designers Charles and Ray Eames], and with their chairs, they were too common, so I didn't use them. I thought the [Origami] chairs were just right for the scene. And, quite frankly, the furniture store who had them, they had multiples." Dwyer confirmed that using the Origami chairs really was more a matter of necessity and accessibility than designer attribution.

When I asked him about any particular stores he remembers using for the show, he mentioned one in Los Angeles called Richards. "The owner was a Trekkie," he said, adding that it had a good selection of contemporary furniture that was right for the show. When I asked him about his recollection of any other specific item he pulled for the show, his eyes lit up and he said, "In

'The Cloud Minders' [Season Three] there was a spray sculpture I really liked, and when I saw it in the store, I felt like I struck gold when I found it!" He said it was exactly right for the episode. Dwyer was eager to say that even on his time off, he would look for art, props, and furniture.

And so concluded my interview with John M. Dwyer, set decorator of *Star Trek*. More biographical information on John Dwyer and his career is provided in the "Season Two" chapter.

Dwyer passed away a year after my interview with him. It was the last interview he gave on his career and his time spent on *Star Trek*. I feel extremely fortunate to have had the opportunity to meet this remarkable man, to whose work, in part, this book is a tribute.

—DAN CHAVKIN, *AUTHOR*

BACKGROUND

In 1964, the first original episode of Gene Roddenberry's creation *Star Trek* was filmed at Desilu Studios. Attempts to market it to the major TV networks were initially unsuccessful. NBC later expressed interest but asked for a second pilot, which was subsequently filmed in mid-1965. *Star Trek*'s ultimate acceptance by NBC for the 1966–1967 TV season—despite this uncertain beginning—launched a franchise that is still going strong more than fifty years later.

Numerous sources are available that chart the incredible birth, evolution, three-year original run, cancellation,[1,2] and spin-off after spin-off of the phenomenal *Star Trek*. That history is not the purpose of this book. Instead, we explore what, up to now, has never been rigorously examined: the approach taken by the creators of *Star Trek* to portray the future. How does one go about depicting the twenty-third century in the middle of the twentieth century in a way that is affordable, practical, and believable?

Paradoxically, *Star Trek* portrayed the future by reaching into the near past: tapping the design genre of Midcentury Modernism.

The birth of modernism itself stretches back into early twentieth century Europe with architects such as Walter Gropius, Ludwig Mies van der Rohe, and Marcel Breuer: representatives of the Bauhaus movement, some of whom emigrated to the United States. Other influential modernist architects who practiced in the US include Richard Neutra and Frank Lloyd Wright. Many of these architects also designed furniture, either as built-ins for the structures they designed or as individual pieces that reflected the look and feel of their architecture.

California became a fertile petri dish for experimentation in architecture and design in the postwar era. Los Angeles itself was ground zero for the Case Study House Program of postwar houses sponsored by the magazine *Arts & Architecture*. Modernist architects such as Eero Saarinen, Craig Ellwood, and Pierre Koenig contributed to this program. The work of Charles and Ray Eames of Los Angeles spanned both architecture and furniture design with their creations, which were fanciful as well as affordable and practical.

Midcentury Modernism as a design era typically is considered to span from the mid-1940s into the 1970s. However, its adoption as a preferred style was by no means universal. In America, at least, typical homeowners were still clinging to the more familiar look of early American and European traditional; furniture manufacturers such as Ethan Allen and Drexel Heritage satisfied that niche. Indeed, for the majority of Middle American households, Midcentury Modernism was strange, cold, somewhat unsettling, and just too futuristic-looking—certainly not a style for everyday living. Hence, for them at least, it had an alien look, which made it the ideal style as a backdrop for science fiction. And through its inherent forward-looking feel, it never appears dated.

This book examines the furnishings, artwork, and props that were chosen for *Star Trek* to help portray both human and nonhuman cultures throughout the far reaches of the galaxy of the future. Behind the scenes, Gene Roddenberry had assembled an incredibly talented creative team of set designers and artists including Carl Biddiscombe, Rolland M. Brooks, John M. Dwyer, Irving A. Feinberg, Walter "Matt" Jefferies, Marvin March, Joseph Stone, and Albert Whitlock. Most of these individuals are no longer with us, but their biographies are included herein.

Because *Star Trek* was on a chronically tight budget, the set designers either had to source items that were readily available in the Los Angeles area or build things quickly—and these items had to channel the twenty-third century, whatever that meant. Fortunately, there was a myriad of Midcentury Modern designers in the US and Europe whose creations fit the bill: Milo Baughman, Bill Curry, Joe Colombo, Paul McCobb, Pierre Paulin, Warren Platner, Eero Saarinen, and Arthur Umanoff, to name just a few. Well-known high-end manufacturers were tapped, including Architectural Pottery, Burke, Chromcraft, Empoli, Kevi, Knoll, and Prescolite.

The methodology for creating this book consisted of binge-watching, excruciatingly intensive freeze-framing and screen-grabbing, and hours of research to track down the identity of selected items with regard to designer and manufacturer. The authors also visited the Star Trek Archive and Product Development facility (managed by ViacomCBS) located in Carson, California, to look for set stills and other relevant documentation. Certain key episodes from all three seasons that depict sophisticated alien cultures, as well as Federation starships and starbases, are dissected. The *Enterprise* itself was a rich source of material: the bridge, the rec room, sickbay, engineering, and various officers' quarters.

Not surprisingly, many episodes of *Star Trek* yielded nothing within our search criteria. Beaming down to a world where inhabitants worship a stone statue named Vaal ("The Apple") would not be expected to yield a high-end piece of Empoli glassware or a Clement Meadmore chair. Neither would parallel-culture nor time-travel episodes that involve Romans ("Bread and Circuses"), gangsters ("A Piece of the Action"), the Wild West ("Spectre of the Gun"), or the Great Depression ("The City on the Edge of Forever"). Other episodes, however, are simply chock-full of modernism—particularly those that portray highly advanced races.

The result is a *Who's Who* of Midcentury Modern Design. Who knew? Some items escaped definitive identification but are nevertheless included due to their beauty and representative style. We have tried to convey how set design articulates with plot, and at one level we discovered that the midcentury item itself becomes a guest star in the episode—with no spoken lines but no less a key component in the story.

The twentieth century meets the twenty-third century in "Tomorrow is Yesterday." While jet pilot Captain John Christopher (Roger Perry) is checking out the *Enterprise* bridge, Uhura is checking out his antiquated space helmet.

Through the liberal use of episode images, this book offers Trek fans an opportunity to revisit some of their favorite episodes, scenes, cast members, and guest stars—but from a different perspective. For Midcentury Modern enthusiasts, the book aspires to be educational, providing biographical and other information on the many designers and manufacturers whose works are represented in *Star Trek*, as well as various vintage advertisements and fun facts.

For those who are both fans and modernists, this book may offer ideas for turning your dwelling into a *Star Trek* set. For that purpose, we include a catalog of featured items at the end of the book. Many of the manufacturers are still in business today, and some of the items featured are still in production. Most may be sourced on the secondary market. You might already own a piece of *Star Trek* in your home and don't know it.

Or perhaps you merely want to acquire a piece of the future, sourced from the past. After all, "Tomorrow Is Yesterday."

—BRIAN MCGUIRE, *AUTHOR*

1 Whitfield SE, Roddenberry G. *The Making of Star Trek*. Ballantine Books, New York NY, 1968.
2 Gerrold D. *The World of Star Trek*. Ballantine Books, New York NY, 1975.

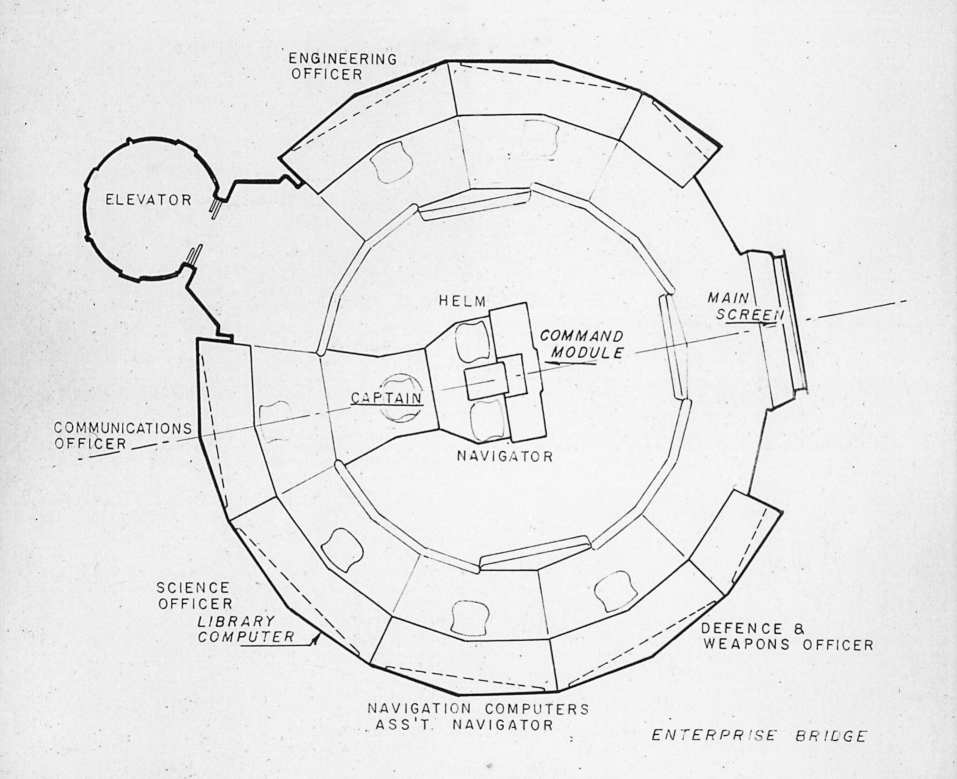

ENGINEERING
OFFICER

ELEVATOR

HELM

COMMAND
MODULE

MAIN
SCREEN

CAPTAIN

COMMUNICATIONS
OFFICER

NAVIGATOR

SCIENCE
OFFICER
LIBRARY
COMPUTER

DEFENCE &
WEAPONS OFFICER

NAVIGATION COMPUTERS
ASS'T. NAVIGATOR

ENTERPRISE BRIDGE

ON THE BRIDGE

LEFT Matt Jefferies' design for the bridge of the *Enterprise*.

The bridge of the *U.S.S. Enterprise* is the fulcrum of the ship's operations, and in a dramatic sense it is the focal point of the series. Designed by Matt Jefferies, each functional station—engineering, communications, science, library computer, defense and weapons, navigation, and viewing screen—holds a strategic location along the perimeter of the circular bridge, articulating with the command module in the center, which consists of the captain's chair and the helmsman's and navigator's stations.

Who would have thought that the products of mid-twentieth-century designers Maurice Burke (inspired by Eero Saarinen) and Arthur Umanoff would be prominently featured on a set representing the bridge of a twenty-third-century starship? Both the crew's chair and the Captain's chair were sourced from furniture suppliers and modified by the production crew to serve their purpose on the bridge. The chairs on which the crew sat were only moderately modified, but the seat that became the captain's chair was transformed almost beyond recognition. These are both described in the ensuing chapter.

The bridge set as it appeared in the episode "This Side of Paradise."

THE BURKE CHAIR

Prominent on the bridge, in the rec room, the briefing room, and other *U.S.S. Enterprise* sets, is the futuristic-looking tulip-style chair, an iconic image of midcentury modern design. Although the version employed in the *Star Trek* series was manufactured by Arkana for the Burke Company of Dallas, Texas, the original Tulip chair was designed by Eero Saarinen, a Finnish American architect famous for designing Dulles International Airport, the TWA Terminal at John F. Kennedy International Airport, the Jefferson National Expansion Memorial (the St. Louis Arch), and the General Motors Technical Center.

Saarinen Tulip chairs by Knoll.

"A chair should not only look well as a piece of sculpture in a room when no one is in it, it should also be a flattering background when someone is in it." —Eero Saarinen

Saarinen, who often collaborated with Charles Eames in both furniture design and architecture, designed his Tulip line of furniture for Knoll Inc., who introduced it in 1956. The chairs and accompanying table each feature a single pedestal leg. The circular base and stem of the chair were enameled aluminum, and the seat and back were molded fiberglass plastic seamlessly joined under the base of the chair. Saarinen, in his attempt to simplify and clarify furniture structure, once remarked:

> "The undercarriage of chairs and tables in a typical interior makes an ugly, confusing, unrestful world. I wanted to clear up the slum of legs. I wanted to make the chair all one thing again."

Saarinen's architecture was known for its free-form, organic lines. Likewise, the furniture he designed echoes the sinuous lines of his architecture. Indeed, the futuristic-looking TWA Terminal at JFK International Airport (designed in 1956) featured his Tulip furniture when it opened in 1962.

Vintage Burke dinette set.

Both pilot episodes used unmodified Burke chairs.

Captain Kirk brawls with a replica of himself in "Whom Gods Destroy" next to a modified Burke chair showing the triangular decals on the back.

In the 1960s, Maurice Burke "borrowed" the original design of Saarinen for his own line of Tulip furniture. Early Burke sets had round bases like the Saarinen line's, but Burke later modified the bases to have a four-pronged "propeller" shape.

The simple, streamlined style of the furniture was ideal for depicting the look of the future. Thus, Desilu Productions acquired models 115 and 116 of the Burke chairs for the pilot episode of its pending science fiction series.

In the two *Star Trek* pilot episodes, "The Cage" and "Where No Man Has Gone Before," the Burke chairs appeared as they had been manufactured. For the ultimate production episodes, however, several modifications were made in accordance with Matt Jefferies' "reimagineering." (See drawings on opposite page.) A vinyl sheath was added to the back in order to increase the height of the chair. One might also hypothesize that the vinyl served to cushion the chairs when they toppled over during Klingon attacks. (For some strange reason they were not bolted to the deck of the bridge.) Additionally, a set of interlocking triangular decals were added to the base of the chair's back.

The *Jetsons*-like look of the furniture served *Star Trek* well, and this line made its appearance on various sets depicting areas of the *Enterprise*—and seemed to be ubiquitous throughout the known galaxy of the twenty-third century on numerous planets and space stations. Several Burke stools appear in the audience room of the civilization that stole Spock's brain in Season Three. A Burke dinette set also appears in the kitchen set on *The Brady Bunch*.

Knoll still markets the Saarinen line of tulip furniture; vintage pieces from both Knoll and Burke are in high demand today on the secondary market.

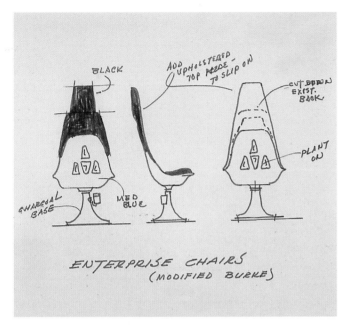

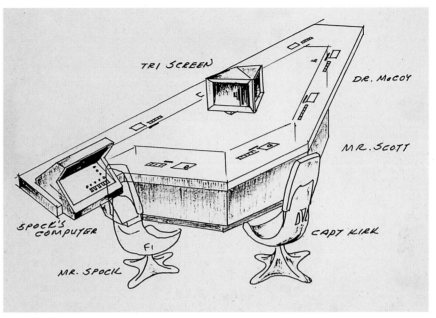

Production sketch of the chair modifications.

Matt Jefferies' sleek version of the *Enterprise* briefing room table also sports two modified Burke chairs.

Lieutenant Uhura in the rec room, surrounded by Burke furniture and an audience, as she sings over the intercom to Kevin Riley in engineering while he is haplessly ingesting milk laced with deadly tetralubrisol.

Captain Kirk's command chair is a perfect example of an everyday object that was ingeniously transformed by the production crew for use on the bridge of the *U.S.S. Enterprise*. While the Burke chairs received only superficial extensions and appliqués, one has difficulty distinguishing the original component of the command chair and tracing it to its designer.

Arthur Umanoff was a prolific but little-known furniture designer. A Pratt Institute graduate, Umanoff began designing furniture in the early 1950s for a company called Product Line Ltd. As a partner in the company, he was involved in all facets of concept and design. Throughout his career, he designed for several other companies, including Shaver Howard, Madison Furniture Industries, Howard Miller Clock Company, the Elton Company, and Boyuer Scott. Umanoff's furniture designs are known for their use of various materials such as wood (including walnut), rattan, and wrought iron. In the 1970s, Umanoff continued designing, for Thonet, Dillingham Manufacturing Company, and David Morgan.

Umanoff's work most relevant to *Star Trek* was for Madison Furniture Industries in Canton, Mississippi. A modular seating unit from his Dimension Twenty-Four collection is shown below and at right. These were commonly used as office reception chairs. The single-chair version (either model nos. 2405 or 4449) with walnut arms and black vinyl upholstery, in production between 1962 and 1968, became the captain's command chair.

Vintage advertisement for Madison Furniture Industries' modular seating unit.

The command chair was constructed in 1964 at Desilu's Culver City Studio for the original pilot episode "The Cage." Matt Jefferies took one of Umanoff's banal-looking lounge chairs with a black vinyl seat and stained wooden armrests, and encased it in a console made of plywood painted battleship gray. The chair was mounted on a wooden pedestal with a spring-loaded swivel. The rectangular base was covered in the same Ozite carpet that covered the entire floor of the bridge. A set of control panels wired for lighting was installed into each of the side arms, which were occasionally switched out to serve the story line. The result became an iconic symbol of authority and adventure.

When the series ended, Paramount dismantled the sets in late 1969 in preparation for scrapping everything. However, the command chair was serendipitously salvaged at that time by an unnamed private individual and was ultimately sold in 2002 at the Profiles in History Bob Justman *Star Trek* Auction in Los Angeles, as Lot No. 175, for $304,750. This original command chair is now on display at the Museum of Pop Culture (previously called the Experience Music Project Museum and the Science Fiction Museum and Hall of Fame) in Seattle.

The chair from which Matt Jefferies created the captain's command chair.

Behind-the-scenes shot from "Where No Man Has Gone Before" showing the command chair in foreground and an unmodified Burke chair in the background. Notice the electrical cord running from the armrest control panel.

The command chair sits serenely amidst a scene of disarray, from "The Way to Eden."

SET DESIGNER & ART DIRECTORS

WALTER M. "MATT" JEFFERIES, set designer and art director of *Star Trek*, was born in Pennsylvania in 1921. As a child, he was heavily influenced by the Buck Rogers and Flash Gordon film serials; these, plus the authors Jules Verne and H.G. Wells, drew him into science fiction. He served in World War II in the Army Air Corps, flying combat missions over Europe and North America, and was a flight-test engineer for four additional years. After the war, he was an illustrator for the Library of Congress.

Jefferies was hired in 1957 as art designer at Warner Bros., working on *The Old Man and the Sea* (1958), *The Wreck of the Mary Deare* (1959), and *The Crowded Sky* (1960). Later, at Desilu Studios, he worked on *The Untouchables* (1959), *Ben Casey* (1961), and *Mission: Impossible* (1966).

Jefferies' creative influence was the driving force in formulating the overall look of *Star Trek*. Working at Desilu when the first *Star Trek* pilot episode presented itself, he was assigned to the project by supervisor Rolland M. Brooks. He designed the exterior of the *Enterprise* and much of the interior, including the bridge and its ergonomic control panels, the captain's command chair, sickbay, engineering, the crews' quarters, the corridors, and the interior of the shuttlecraft. He designed many props for the show, including the phaser weapons. He also designed the Klingon battle cruiser. In his honor, the vertical crawl shafts allowing maintenance access between decks were termed Jefferies tubes.

Following his *Star Trek* work, Jefferies continued in art direction and set design, contributing to *Love, American Style*, *Little House on the Prairie*, and *Dallas*, as well as the feature movie *Catch-22*. In the late 1970s, Jefferies worked with NASA engineers in designing the prototype for the first reusable space shuttle, aptly named the *Enterprise*, and was present at the test landing. Jefferies owned and flew his own plane and was a member of the Aviation/Space Writers' Association and the American Aviation Historical Society. Jefferies died in Los Angeles in 2003.

ROLLAND M. BROOKS, art director on *Star Trek*, was born in Tacoma, Washington, in 1907. His work in production design and art direction spanned three decades.

Brooks was the supervising art director at Desilu Studios, where he worked for twelve years. Most of his work was in television, including, notably, *The Untouchables* (1959–63), *The Andy Griffith Show* (1961), *The Danny Thomas Show* (1961), *The Real McCoys* (1961–63), *Ben Casey* (1961–66), *The Lucy Show,* and the first two seasons of *Here's Lucy* (1968–70).

At the time the *Star Trek* pilot was being proposed in 1964, Brooks's workload prevented him from involvement in "The Cage," which he delegated to colleague Matt Jefferies. He did, however, do the art direction for the second pilot, "Where No Man Has Gone Before," on the basis of which *Star Trek* was picked up by NBC. Brooks worked closely with Jefferies during the entire first season. When, in 1967, Lucille Ball sold Desilu to Gulf+Western (which had recently acquired Paramount Pictures), Brooks decided to become an independent contractor, leaving *Star Trek*, after the fourth episode in the second season. Meanwhile, Desilu went on to become the television production unit of Paramount.

All told, Brooks contributed to thirty-four episodes of *Star Trek*, including "The Corbomite Maneuver," "The Man Trap," The Conscience of the King", "Court Martial," "A Taste of Armageddon," "Operation -- Annihilate!," and "Metamorphosis"—the episodes most heavily laden with midcentury modern decor. His most recognizable *Star Trek* contribution was his design for the Guardian on "The City on the Edge of Forever," a doughnut-shaped structure forming the portal to other time periods.

Other notable activity during and after *Star Trek* included art direction on *Hogan's Heroes* and *Mission: Impossible*. His last project was the 1973 TV movie *The Bait*. Brooks died in Monterey, California, in 1998.

SEASON ONE

THE CAGE

Season N/A • **Production Sequence** 01 • **Air Date** N/A • **Stardate** Unknown
Art Directors Walter M. "Matt" Jefferies, Pato Guzman • **Set Decorator** Franz Bachelin • **Property Masters** Wah Chang, Jim Danforth

SYNOPSIS

On their way to the Vega colony after a hostile encounter on Rigel VII, the *Enterprise*, commanded by Captain Christopher Pike (played by Jeffrey Hunter), receives a radio distress signal, ostensibly from the Earth vessel *SS Columbia,* which disappeared eighteen years ago. The signal leads the crew to the fourth planet of the Talos system, which appears to be barren—until they discover human survivors. As it turns out, all is an illusion; there is no camp of survivors. The native Talosians are all that remain of a former great civilization destroyed by war. At the expense of physical evolution, they have developed their mental powers to enable themselves to read and manipulate the minds of others. They had deliberately lured the *Enterprise* to Talos IV

in an attempt to repopulate the planet using (as breeding stock) Vina—the one true survivor of the crash—and her ideal image of a mate: Captain Pike.

Accomplished actress Susan Oliver offers a haunting performance as the human castaway Vina, who has been psychologically tormented by the Talosians and forced to entice Pike to join her in her world of illusion.

Viewers of "The Cage" are treated to their first glimpses of the *U.S.S. Enterprise.* Only a handful of *Enterprise* sets were built for this pilot: the bridge, a corridor, Pike's quarters, the transporter room, and a briefing room. Additionally, the overall "look" of the *Enterprise* in terms of furnishings had not yet been completely realized.

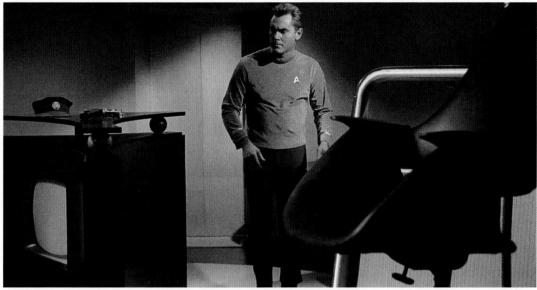

Captain Pike's living quarters.

▶ SWIVEL CHAIR FOR MADISON FURNITURE INDUSTRIES · USA · 1960s
DESIGNER: ARTHUR UMANOFF

After making a painful decision about whether to investigate the radio distress signal, Pike heads for his quarters, pensive and disillusioned. As he passes through his living area to flop down on his bed, we see a sharp, futuristic-looking chair by midcentury designer Arthur Umanoff. The previous chapter, "On the Bridge," presents biographical information on Umanoff as well as his other more notable contribution to *Star Trek*—the seat that formed the basis of the captain's command chair.

Umanoff's swivel chair in a vintage furniture catalog.

Umanoff swivel chair

Upon the abduction of Pike by the Talosians down on the planet, *Enterprise* officers, led by Number One, convene in the conference room to strategize. Unmodified Burke chairs encircle the conference table; these were standard issue for crew members on the Bridge and throughout the *Enterprise*. (The origins of this tulip-style furniture in Eero Saarinen's designs are also discussed in the "On the Bridge" chapter.) Likewise present in the foreground of the conference room is the same Umanoff chair seen in Captain Pike's quarters.

In a rare production still from the set of "The Cage" (below), actress Susan Oliver chats with Gene Roddenberry, director Robert Butler, and producer Robert H. Justman prior to shooting the picnic scene with Jeffrey Hunter. Visible in the background is the Albert Whitlock matte painting representing twenty-third-century Mojave, California; this and other matte paintings used in the series are discussed in the "Futurist Architecture" chapter.

> "THE HUMAN RACE IS A REMARKABLE CREATURE, ONE WITH GREAT POTENTIAL, AND I HOPE THAT *STAR TREK* HAS HELPED TO SHOW US WHAT WE CAN BE IF WE BELIEVE IN OURSELVES AND OUR ABILITIES."
>
> —GENE RODDENBERRY

⟨THE CORBOMITE MANEUVER

Season 1 • **Production Sequence** 03 • **Air Date** November 10, 1966 • **Stardate** 1512.2 • **Art Directors** Rolland M. Brooks (as Roland M. Brooks), Walter M. "Matt" Jefferies • **Set Decorator** Carl F. Biddiscombe • **Property Master** Irving A. Feinberg

SYNOPSIS

While exploring an uncharted sector of the galaxy, the *Enterprise* is forced to destroy a threatening marker buoy. As a result of this action, a gigantic alien ship, the *Fesarius*, arrives, commanded by an evil-looking alien named Balok, who condemns the *Enterprise* as a trespasser and threatens to destroy it. Captain Kirk bluffs Balok by invoking an imaginary destructive substance called corbomite. The resulting tension tests the nerve and resolve of young, untried navigator, Lieutenant Bailey. Three *Enterprise* crew members beam

over to the alien vessel to discover the real Balok to be a diminutive, child-like creature (played by a seven-year-old Clint Howard), who welcomes them aboard and offers the crew his favorite drink, tranya, to toast their meeting. Balok explains that he was only testing the intentions of the *Enterprise* and desires to host a human ambassador, and Bailey volunteers.

RIGHT "We must drink. This is tranya. I hope you relish it as much as I."

MODULAR STANDING LANTERN FOR ARCHITECTURAL POTTERY · USA · CIRCA 1951

DESIGNER: MALCOM LELAND

After falling for the bluff, Balok welcomes Kirk, Dr. McCoy, and Bailey aboard his ship. Standing prominently beside Balok is a Malcolm Leland–designed floor lantern. The prop, with its pulsing, colored lights, acts as Balok's command tower, through which he controls his ship.

Leland, prolific in ceramics and sculpture, opened his own ceramics studio at the age of thirty-one. He studied at the Yale School of Art, the University of Southern California, and the Jepson Art Institute in Los Angeles. Consisting of clay, aluminum, bronze, and cast concrete, Leland's works were most associated with the Los Angeles company Architectural Pottery, founded in 1950. It was for Architectural Pottery that he licensed a grouping of planters, birdhouses, and other home accessories. Leland was commissioned by several modernist architects, including Richard Neutra, to create large cast-concrete structures. Sites of those sculptures include the Los Angeles County Hall of Records, the American Cement Company Building, and the San Diego Museum of Art. Leland also taught at Chouinard Art Institute.

Malcolm Leland's candle lantern.

Appearing in the background on the right is the floor lantern, serving double duty in McCoy's seldom-seen laboratory from "Operation -- Annihilate!"

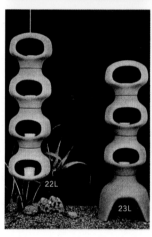

22L

23L

Images from vintage advertisement for Malcolm Leland's candle lanterns from the Architectural Pottery Catalog 1964.

Designed as a lantern or totem, the device was intended to have candles placed inside each modular vessel. Cast in terra-cotta, the 23-L lantern model is a stackable piece of varying sizes produced by Architectural Pottery. The lantern was also offered in hanging and wall versions. Balok's control module was painted black, possibly to appear more ominous and imposing. With a simple touch of the device, however, Balok serves the tranya to his *Enterprise* guests.

Architectural Pottery was formed by husband and wife Max and Rita Lawrence. Filling a need for a modernist expression in outdoor and indoor pottery, the Lawrences worked with a host of artisans, all of whom received authorship and royalties for their designs. Over its thirty-plus-year history, Architectural Pottery sold to many designers and noted modernist architects throughout the country. Eventually, the pottery became synonymous with the midcentury modern aesthetic.

"TO BE DIFFERENT IS NOT NECESSARILY TO BE UGLY; TO HAVE A DIFFERENT IDEA IS NOT NECESSARILY TO BE WRONG. THE WORST POSSIBLE THING IS FOR ALL OF US TO BEGIN TO LOOK AND TALK AND ACT AND THINK ALIKE."

—GENE RODDENBERRY

 THE MAN TRAP

Season 1 • **Production Sequence** 06 • **Air Date** September 8, 1966 • **Stardate** 1513.1
Art Director Rolland M. Brooks • **Set Decorator** Carl F. Biddiscombe • **Property Master** Irving A. Feinberg

SYNOPSIS

The first season of *Star Trek* opened with this episode of galactic archeology, lost love, and a metaphor for the extinct buffalo. Nancy Crater (Jeanne Bal), wife and partner of an archaeologist on Planet M-113—and an old flame of Dr. McCoy's—actually turns out to be a hairy, shape-shifting, salt-craving creature that suctions all the sodium chloride from its victims' bodies, leaving them horribly disfigured and quite dead. Down on the planet and later loose on the *Enterprise*, the creature kills several crew members and threatens Lieutenants Uhura and Sulu, and Yeoman Janice Rand, in its insatiable quest for salt. To save the captain's life,

McCoy must struggle to reconcile what he feels with what he sees and knows to be true.

This episode contains a poignant character-defining moment between Mr. Spock and Uhura, when the latter unsuccessfully attempts to engage the former in superficial romantic banter about lazy evenings on Vulcan when the moon is full.

Spock: "Vulcan has no moon, Miss Uhura."
Uhura: "I'm not surprised, Mister Spock."

Janice Rand about to be accosted by the salt vampire in the form of crewman Green as he attempts to grab the salt shaker.

▶ SALT & PEPPER SHAKERS FOR WÜRTTEMBERGISCHE METALLWARENFABRIK · GERMANY · 1952-53
DESIGNER: WILHELM WAGENFELD

Assuming the identity of murdered crewman Green, the salt vampire is beamed aboard the *Enterprise*. The salt-deprived impostor first confronts Rand carrying Sulu's food tray. It is our first glimpse of the hourglass-shaped shakers. Since salt was the theme of the episode, the dramatic need of the scene required that these be made of glass to show what was motivating the creature. He follows Rand to the botany section of the ship's life sciences department, where Sulu awaits his food.

Industrial designer Wilhelm Wagenfeld was a student at the Bauhaus art school under László Moholy-Nagy. At an early age, he apprenticed in a silver factory. Working in glass and metal, he designed consumer products for the companies Jenaer Glaswerk Schott & Gen, Braun, and Rosenthal. Later, he became the design director at Württembergische Metallwarenfabrik in Stuttgart. A number of his designs are in still production.

Originally manufactured in the early 1950s, the Wagenfeld shakers are timeless in design. An alternate set of salt shakers had been procured for the sequence with Rand and the salt vampire but were rejected for this episode, as they were too futuristic-looking (and also were not transparent glass) and were later recycled as some of McCoy's operating tools. (See the "Set Decoration, Props, and Fashion" chapter.)

Close-up of the shakers on the tray that Janice Rand delivers to Sulu in the botany section of the *Enterprise*.

Wilhelm Wagenfeld.

In a comic publicity still from NBC, actress Jeanne Bal finally satisfies her desire for salt

"I see. So, naturally, when I'm lonely, I think of you."

John Follis planters, from the Architectural Pottery catalog.

▶ **CERAMIC PLANTER FOR ARCHITECTURAL POTTERY · USA · 1951**

DESIGNER: JOHN FOLLIS

Uhura almost becomes the next victim of the salt vampire: now in the guise of a Swahili-speaking crewman. She is saved by the sudden opening of the botany section door as Yeoman Rand exits, revealing a tall, exotic plant in a piece from Architectural Pottery designed by John Follis.

Follis studied at the ArtCenter in Pasadena, California (later called the ArtCenter College of Design) as well as the California School of Art in Los Angeles. It was under the guidance of instructor LaGardo Tackett at the latter when Follis met classmate Rex Goode. What began as a class assignment with Goode grew into a business designing ceramic planters for Architectural Pottery. Primarily known as an accomplished graphic designer, Follis opened his own firm in 1960. He also designed numerous covers for the important magazine *Arts & Architecture*. He taught at the ArtCenter, the University of California, Los Angeles (UCLA), and California State University, Los Angeles, and authored the seminal book *Architectural Signing and Graphics*.

The planter bearing the designation CP-21, is also known as "the Tire" due to its appearance. It is fitting that the botany section of the *Enterprise* would feature a planter made by a company that defined California living in the 1950s and '60s, as *Star Trek* was filmed entirely in Southern California. The Follis-designed "Tire" planter was offered in various sizes, as featured in the Architectural Pottery catalog from 1964.

THE CONSCIENCE OF THE KING

Season 1 • **Production Sequence** 13 • **Air Date** December 8, 1966 • **Stardate** 2817.6

Art Directors Rolland M. Brooks, Walter M. "Matt" Jefferies • **Set Decorator** Marvin March • **Property Master** Irving A. Feinberg

SYNOPSIS

Macbeth, *Hamlet*, and poisoned milk converge in this story of Shakespearean actor Anton Karidian (Arnold Moss), who is suspected of being Kodos the Executioner—the ex-governor of Tarsus IV who, twenty years previously during a food shortage, slaughtered half the colonists in order to save the other half. Kodos disappeared thereafter and, tellingly, Anton Karidian's history began at about the same time. Those who can identify Kodos are being knocked off one by one, with the Shakespearean acting company always in the vicinity. Dr. Thomas Leighton, scientist, old friend of Captain Kirk, and one of these eyewitnesses, issues an emergency distress call to the *Enterprise* from Planet Q to report his suspicions of Karidian, and immediately becomes the next murder victim. His mysterious death leaves only Kirk and Lieutenant Kevin Riley (Bruce Hyde) on the *Enterprise* as the remaining eyewitnesses to Kodos.

Barbara Anderson offers a riveting performance as the beautiful Lenore Karidian, disturbed daughter of the suspect. Ms. Anderson appears above in seventeenth-century Shakespearean garb holding a twenty-third-century phaser—a dramatic study in contrasts. Lieutenant Uhura gives a show-stopping performance singing "Beyond Antares" to Riley over the intercom as he is drinking milk poisoned with tetralubrisol by the unknown assassin.

▶ COLUMNLITE MODELS G & C-4 FOR DESIGN LINE INC. · USA · CIRCA 1965

DESIGNER: BILL CURRY

Dr. Leighton's smartly decorated house features a slick midcentury aesthetic—a de facto gallery including modernist abstract paintings, Brutalist wall sculptures, and high-end furnishings. To the left, behind Captain Kirk in the photograph below, is a towering, thoroughly modern model G Columnlite by Bill Curry with its strong verticality.

Lighting designer Bill Curry founded his own lighting company, Design Line Inc., with his wife, Jacqueline, in 1962 in El Segundo, California. A graduate of the Art Center, Curry got his start as an art director for the Ramo-Wooldridge Company, a precursor to TRW Inc. (See the "Futurist Architecture" chapter.) Curry's lighting designs received many accolades, including Best Lamps of the Year by *Industrial Design* magazine; he was also named

one of California's Leading Designers by the *Los Angeles Times*. His designs were also showcased numerous times as part of the Pasadena Museum of California Art's annual *California Design* exhibits. Utilitarian and practical, Curry's lamps pioneered the concept of the bare bulb, eliminating the lampshade altogether.

DESIGN LINE, INCORPORATED, EL SEGUNDO, CALIFORNIA

Design Line Inc. advertisement.

"He is Kodos. I'm sure of it . . . I remember him . . . that voice . . ."

A smaller table version of the Columnlite, model C-4, is visible in the living room where Kirk and Lenore become acquainted. Curry is perhaps better known for his Stemlite mushroom lamp, which was adapted by the Laurel Lamp Company for its own version.

Bill Curry, photographed by Max Eckart in Curry's Design Line outlet store.

"So, Lady MacBeth . . . interesting. What's your next move?"

▶ SWIVEL ROCKER CLUB CHAIR FOR THAYER COGGIN · USA · 1960s
DESIGNER: MILO BAUGHMAN

The image above of Captain Kirk at the reception for the Shakespearean act-ing company in the Leightons' house is packed with items of interest. Visible outside the window is the space colony on Planet Q as envisioned by matte painter Albert Whitlock. (See the "Futurist Architecture" chapter.) Visible in the lower right is a metal foliage sculpture discussed below. Other abstract table and wall art complement the furnishings. In a corner in Dr. Leighton's living space is a swivel club chair by noted designer Milo Baughman. Uphol-stered in lush orange-brown fabric, it emanates sophistication and comfort.

Baughman was one of the great leading designers of his generation. Having attended the ArtCenter and the Chinouard Art Institute after serving in World War II, he worked for Frank Brothers, an influential modernist furniture store. In 1947, he founded Milo Baughman Design Inc. Six years later, Baughman began his fifty-year collaboration with Thayer Coggin Inc. He also designed for sev-eral other companies, including Glenn of California, Pacific Iron, Mode Furni-ture, Drexel, and Directional Industries. But it was his association with Thayer Coggin, which continued until his death, through which he was most famous. Baughman designed many iterations of the swivel chair owned by Dr. Leigh-ton—plush, rotating, and usually covered in luxurious textiles.

Baughman's designs were seen in many celebrity homes.

▶ SNAIL & FOLIAGE BRASS SCULPTURE FOR ARTISAN · USA · 1966
DESIGNER: CURTIS JERÉ

Dr. Leighton's impeccable taste does not save him from the same fate as most of the other Kodos eyewitnesses. Captain Kirk and Lenore discover his body after they leave the reception for a walk. With his wife, Martha, sitting solemnly by Leighton's body, we see in the foreground a Curtis Jeré metal sculpture depicting a snail and foliage (also visible to the right of Kirk in the photograph above).

Curtis Jeré, the professional name of Jerry Fels and his brother-in-law partner Kurt Freiler, founded the company Artisan House in Los Angeles in 1963. As further described in the "The *Enterprise* Incident," Jeré's practice was known for producing free-standing and wall-mounted sculptures of various animals, street scenes, and foliage using a variety of materials such as brass, copper, and bronze. Representations from nature were common in Curtis Jere's work.

Barely visible behind Lenore at Leighton's reception (shown on the opposite page) is some kind of exotic orchid-like plant with a metallic sheen in a white rectangular planter. To the left of this is a pencil cactus (genus *Euphorbia*), common in Southern California landscapes and apparently indigenous to Planet Q.

COURT MARTIAL

Season 1 • **Production Sequence** 15 • **Air Date** February 2, 1967 • **Stardate** 2947.3
Art Directors Rolland M. Brooks, Walter M. "Matt" Jefferies • **Set Decorator** Marvin March • **Property Master** Irving A. Feinberg

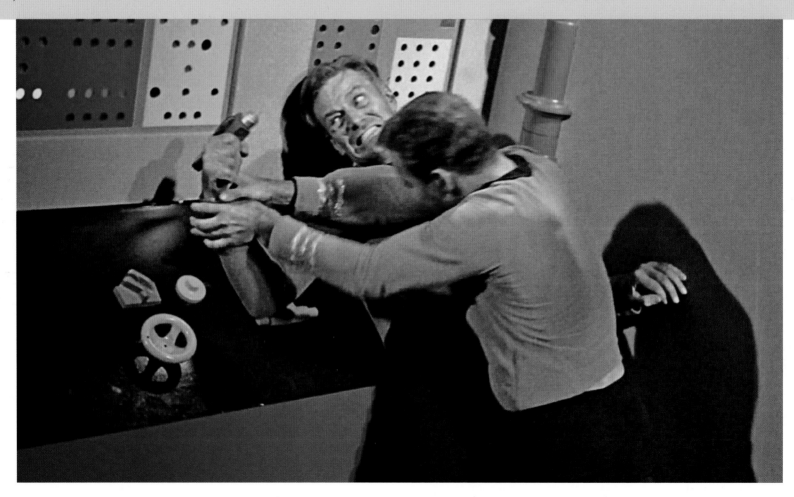

SYNOPSIS

During an ion storm, records officer Ben Finney is taking readings in an external pod. Captain Kirk, assuming that Finney had already vacated, jettisons the pod for the safety of the ship and Finney is ostensibly lost. Later on, at Starbase 11, a formal Starfleet inquiry is instigated to determine whether Kirk jettisoned the pod prematurely: prior to or after the red alert—especially since Kirk and Finney had a history of mutual enmity. Kirk's accuser: the ship's computer log, which clearly shows his finger pushing the jettison button during the yellow alert. To further confound the situation, the prosecuting attorney, Areel Shaw (played by Joan Marshall) is an old flame of Kirk's. Veteran actor Elisha Cook, Jr., plays defense attorney Samuel T. Cogley in this courtroom drama.

We visit Starbase 11 for the first time (also featured in "The Menagerie"); it is discussed further in the "Futurist Architecture" chapter.

From a Prescolite catalog page.

▶ HANGING PENDANT LIGHT FOR PRESCOLITE · USA · 1960s

After a heated confrontation with Kirk's peers in the lounge of Starbase 11, he returns to his quarters to find an eccentric lawyer who has taken up residence there. Bracketing a black modernist sofa (covered entirely in law books) is a pair of pendant lights created by Prescolite.

Prescolite was founded in 1944 by Pres Jones and Wally Runswick in a Berkeley, California, garage. Together they introduced one of the first recessed downlights. The company moved its headquarters to nearby San Leandro in 1963. In 1966, the company introduced mercury-vapor downlights with patented Silent Pak ballasts. Prescolite is still one of the leading designers of recessed, surface, and track lighting for both residential and industrial uses.

Made of hand-blown smoked glass in a cylindrical shape casting soft light, the hanging lamps we see in "Court Martial" were part of the company's mid-1960s Holiday pendant line. These were offered in an assortment of satin silk colors in unusual futuristic shapes. The line's catalog copy read: "A gay and colorful grouping of pendant forms designed and executed in hand-blown combinations of colored glass as well as exquisite satin opal glass." A perfect fit for Starbase 11.

45

Several interesting mid-century pieces in this episode elude identification. In Kirk's quarters on Starbase 11 is a unique black sofa replete with angular shapes and distinguished by the fact that the back of the sofa is a separate piece mounted on the wall. This was possibly constructed by the set designers and was also used in Dr. McCoy's office in the Season Three episode "For the World is Hollow and I Have Touched the Sky."

Also in the same room are several black swivel chairs with rounded backs sitting on a propeller-style base—a design similar to that of the Burke chair. These are undoubtedly commercial products but are from an unknown designer and manufacturer.

Visible in the courtroom during Kirk's trial (as shown in the photograph at right) are some unique tables, one for the prosecution and one for the defense. The legs are Z-shaped, creating a feeling of forward thrust to the tables. It is posited that these were built by the set designers. They were also used on the *Enterprise* in the Season Two episode "By Any Other Name."

Two scenes of this episode take place in the lounge of Starbase 11. In addition to the decorative screen visible through the entryway behind Kirk is an interesting set of cut-out apertures behind the bar, both of which provide visual interest to the set.

Other items of interest in this visually rich episode are discussed elsewhere in the book: the Starbase 11 matte shot (see the "Futurist Architecture" chapter), and Dr. McCoy's cardiac monitor, so critical to the plot (see the "Set Decoration, Props, and Fashion" chapter.)

A TASTE OF ARMAGEDDON

Season 1 • **Production Sequence** 23 • **Air Date** February 23, 1967 • **Stardate** 3192.1
Art Directors Rolland M. Brooks, Walter M. "Matt" Jefferies • **Set Decorator** Marvin March • **Property Masters** Irving A. Feinberg

SYNOPSIS

The *Enterprise* arrives unwelcomed in a solar system engaged in a 500-year-old computerized war, with simulated strikes and retaliation—but with real consequences, as those who are, according to the virtual results, deemed casualties, are marched into disintegration chambers and vaporized. While the *Enterprise* is orbiting Eminiar VII, the adjacent planet Vendikar stages an attack, and the entire *Enter-*prise crew are consequently included in the official death tally. Captain Kirk and Mr. Spock must convince their hostess Mea 3 (played by Barbara Babcock in the first of her two appearances on *Star Trek*) and the planet's leaders that their tidy, sanitized game is merely masking the horrible reality of war—and that the countless deaths just might be avoided through diplomacy.

Our first glimpse of Eminiar VII is at the beam-down site at the gates to the city. The crisp, linear cityscape looming in the distance (see the matte painting in the "Futurist Architecture" chapter) does little to reveal the war that has raged for centuries between Eminiar VII and Vendikar. The harsh, jagged texture of the artwork that predominates on Eminiar is likewise paradoxical for such an advanced culture, perhaps reflecting its disquiet as a result of the ongoing conflict.

▶ HANGING LAMP FOR FELDMAN LIGHTING COMPANY · USA · 1960s
DESIGNER: TOM GREENE

Once the landing party is welcomed to Eminiar VII, they are almost immediately made prisoners as casualties of the computerized war. The crew are, however, able to lounge around in a tastefully decorated detention area—a virtual showroom of midcentury pieces that includes one of several variations of a hanging Tom Greene Brutalist torch-cut lamp.

Originally owning a dental-prosthetic laboratory, Greene, a UCLA dental school graduate, employed tools and techniques he had used in his laboratory to make jewelry and fixtures. He also used the lost-wax process—by which molten metal is poured into a mold to create a wax model. Later, he made larger sculptural pieces using an oxyacetylene torch to create designs of flora and figures from brass, copper, and bronze. With these pieces, Greene forged a relationship with the retailer Monteverde Young. He then began making lighting fixtures in the Brutalist style for the Feldman Lighting Company and Lightolier. His commissions included lighting for Las Vegas casinos, film studios, hotels, Walt Disney, and Princess Cruise Ship Lines.

STONEWARE CERAMIC VESSEL FOR ARCHITECTURAL POTTERY · USA · CIRCA 1964
DESIGNER: DAVID CRESSEY

Visible in the foreground of the detention room (see the photograph on the previous page) is a stoneware vessel made by David Cressey for Architectural Pottery. The walls of the room are adorned with other Brutalist pieces, typical of the style that defines the city.

A Los Angeles native, Cressey studied ceramics at USC under ceramicist Vivika Heino and continued his studies at UCLA, where he earned his master's degree in 1956. Cressey then taught at UCLA and Mount Saint Mary's College in Los Angeles as chairman of the Art Department. Shortly thereafter, he joined Architectural Pottery as an artist-in-residence where he worked until 1965 and for whom he created many designs for planters and various other custom vessels. Cressey's line of stoneware with textured patterns was eventually called the Pro/Artisan collection.

From Architectural Pottery catalog.

Barely visible on the right is a grouping of Warren Platner furniture: two chairs and a coffee table.

▶ CHAIRS AND COFFEE TABLE FOR KNOLL INC. · USA · 1966
DESIGNER: WARREN PLATNER

After Kirk's escape from the detention room, he confronts the deceptive and devious Councilman Anan 7, whose quarters—similar to the detention room—are replete with opulent furnishings and fanciful wall sculptures. Anan 7's seating area contains an entire set of Warren Platner's "Platner Collection" furniture: a glass-and-metal coffee table surrounded by lounge chairs in red and purple.

Platner graduated from the Cornell University School of Architecture in 1941. He later worked in some of the most prestigious offices, including those of Raymond Loewy, Kevin Roche, and Eero Saarinen. In Saarinen's architectural firm, he worked on Dulles International Airport, the Lincoln Center, and the dormitories at Yale University. Platner opened his own design office in 1967.

In 1966, Platner released his groundbreaking line of multiple chrome rod-based chairs, lounge chairs, ottomans, and tables called the Platner Collection, manufactured and marketed by Knoll Inc. These highly sculptural pieces were complicated to make and consisted of over one thousand welds. At the time of their conception, the Platner line exemplified the space-age aesthetic, with its multiple-rod structure and curved lines. The chairs and table, which almost appear to float, are still in production today. Platner's work as an interior designer included the Georg Jensen showroom, the Windows of the World restaurant atop the World Trade Center, and Water Tower Place in Chicago.

▶ STEMLITE MODEL C-3 LAMP FOR DESIGN LINE INC. · USA · CIRCA 1965
DESIGNER: BILL CURRY

Beneath a prominent wall sculpture in Anan 7's quarters is a Bill Curry mushroom lamp on a stem base.

A graduate of the ArtCenter, lighting designer Bill Curry got his start as an art director for the Ramo-Wooldridge Company. Curry founded his own lighting company, Design Line Inc., with his wife, Jacqueline, in 1962 in El Segundo, California. His designs were showcased numerous times at the Museum of California Art's annual *California Design* exhibits. More on Bill Curry may be found in the episode "The Conscience of the King."

"You are a barbarian . . . a killer first, a builder second, a hunter, a warrior, and let's be honest, a murderer. That is our joint heritage, is it not?"

The Curry lamp at the far left inspired the famous mushroom lamp marketed by the Laurel Company—said by some to be a metaphor for a mushroom cloud in a nuclear explosion.

"What kind of monster are you?" "I'm a barbarian. You said it yourself."

▶ KE3-1 SWIVEL CHAIR FOR KEVI · DENMARK · 1960s
DESIGNERS: JORGEN RASMUSSEN AND ERIK MOLLER

Five Rasmussen and Moller swivel chairs on casters appear in the chamber for the members of Eminiar VII's High Council. The yellow chair in the middle with armrests denotes the position for the highest-ranking member, Anan 7. The office chairs are utilitarian and practical. The more popular and widely used version of the chair was simple in its design, with only a thin back rest and seat joined by a metal rod all atop a four-star base on casters.

Jorgen Rasmussen was born in Odense, Denmark, in 1931. In 1955, he graduated from the Royal Danish Academy of Fine Arts, and in 1957 he and his brother started their own design studio. His collaboration with Erik Moller resulted in the design of the multipurpose home and office work chair for the company Kevi. Rasmussen invented the double-wheel caster for which he was awarded the Danish design award the ID Prize.

Moller was a Danish architect who worked under famous architect and designer Arne Jacobsen. Together, they designed a number of public works in Denmark, including several town halls.

"Won't you join me for a drink, Captain?" "I didn't come here to drink." Note on the right another example of Tom Greene's torch-cut lamps.

▶ TALL BOTTLE FOR BODA GLASSWORKS · SWEDEN · 1960s
DESIGNER: ERIK HOGLUND

A further reflection of his seemingly impeccable taste, Anan 7's quarters contains an Erik Hoglund tall-necked bottle made by Boda Glassworks, which he uses as a liquor decanter. It sits beside a very striking piece of Brutalist sculpture.

Hoglund was born in 1932 in Karlskrona, Sweden. His education began at the Swedish School of Arts, Crafts, and Design in Stockholm. In 1953, Hoglund was hired by Boda, where he worked for the next 20 years. (Since 1898, the company has enlisted many artisans to create its distinctive line of famous glassware.)

Soon after, he traveled to Italy and Greece. Cultivating his own style, Hoglund created more unusual shapes, some of which were based on prehistoric cultures. He also introduced air bubbles within his glass forms. In the 1960s, Hoglund began making pieces in forged iron and other materials. After leaving Boda in 1973, Erik Hoglund founded his own smithery. Years later, in the 1980s, Hoglund returned to making glass objects.

Also found in Anan 7's quarters is an alternate version of the Tom Greene hanging Brutalist lamp, seen to the right of Kirk and Anan 7.

SET DECORATORS

CARL F. BIDDISCOMBE, set decorator on *Star Trek*, was born in New Brunswick, Canada, in 1924. His career in Hollywood spanned four decades. Prior to his work on *Star Trek*, he was set decorator on numerous TV shows including *The Rifleman* (1959–60), *Sea Hunt* (1961), *Bus Stop* (1961–62), and 84 episodes of *Perry Mason* (1963–66).

Biddiscombe was set decorator for eight *Star Trek* episodes in Season One: "The Corbomite Maneuver," "The Man Trap," "Charlie X," "What are Little Girls Made Of?" "Mudd's Women," "The Enemy Within," "The Naked Time," and "Balance of Terror."

Other activities during and after his work on *Star Trek* included set decoration for *The Invaders*, *That Girl*, *The Mothers-in-Law*, *Mannix*, *Cannon*, *Barnaby Jones*, and numerous other TV shows into the 1980s. Biddiscombe was nominated for two Academy Awards in Art Direction for the movies *Gaily, Gaily* (1969) and *Tora! Tora! Tora!* (1970). He died in Laguna Niguel in 2000.

MARVIN MARCH, set decorator on *Star Trek*, was born in 1930. His career in set and art direction spanned four decades. He worked on the first season of *Star Trek* as set decorator, contributing to episodes including "The Conscience of the King," "Court Martial," "A Taste of Armageddon," "Operation -- Annihilate!," and "The Menagerie."

Achievements after his *Star Trek* years include art direction on the movies *The Sunshine Boys*, *The Turning Point*, *California Suite*, *Annie*, and *Addams Family Values*—all of which earned him Academy Award nominations. He retired in 1998, and in 2005 he received a Lifetime Achievement Award from the Set Decorators Society of America.

⬡ OPERATION—ANNIHILATE!

Season 1 • **Production Sequence** 29 • **Air Date** April 13, 1967 • **Stardate** 3287.2
Art Directors Rolland Brooks, Walter M. "Matt" Jefferies • **Set Decorator** Marvin March • **Property Masters** Irving A. Feinberg, Wah Chang

SYNOPSIS

The *Enterprise* rushes to the planet Deneva, whose solar system has experienced an outbreak of mass insanity; the urgency is amplified by the fact that Captain Kirk's brother Sam (a research biologist) and his family are residents. The planet has been invaded by deadly neural parasites resembling patties of vomit. And they fly! Each creature corresponds to a single cell of a multicelled organism endeavoring to take over the planet. By implanting stingers into their victims, the creatures overcome the nervous system, forcing the host to carry out its will. Kirk, Mr. Spock, and Dr. McCoy must figure out how to eradicate the organism without having to nuke the entire planet along with the one million surviving inhabitants, including Kirk's nephew Peter (Craig Hundley).

This episode made extensive use of on-location shooting, both exteriors and interiors. Viewers are treated to an architectural tour of what was then the TRW Space and Defense Park in Redondo Beach, California (now the headquarters of Northrup Grumman Aerospace Systems). Designed by Albert C. Martin and Associates, the newly completed futuristic complex made an ideal setting for Deneva; an exterior shot of UCLA's Schoenberg School of Music was also used in this episode. Both are discussed further in the "Futurist Architecture" chapter.

"They're here! They're here! Please—keep them away!"

► HIGH-BACK LOUNGE CHAIR FOR SELIG · USA · 1960s
DESIGNER: LAWRENCE PEABODY

After beaming down to the planet and being accosted by some crazed inhabitants of Deneva, Captain Kirk and crew hear screams from a nearby building housing Sam Kirk's laboratory, which happens to be tricked out with some fine midcentury pieces. They discover Kirk's sister-in-law, Aurelan, who has gone completely mental. In the foreground is a green Lawrence Peabody lounge chair into which Aurelan collapses. The chair is part of Peabody's Holiday series model 576, manufactured by Selig.

Born in Massachusetts, Peabody attended the Rhode Island School of Design after serving in the navy. Peabody also studied in Copenhagen, at the Royal Academy of Fine Arts. In 1955, he opened his own design firm, Lawrence Peabody and Associates, where he operated both as an architect and an interior designer. His clients included Kohler, Sears Roebuck, and Richardson Brothers. In 1960, Peabody purchased a home in Port-Au-Prince, Haiti, where he befriended Dewitt Peters, the founder of Haiti's Le Centre d'Art, where he became head director. The center was instrumental in promoting local Haitian artists. Peabody eventually brought to the United States a collection of one-of-a-kind furniture made by Haitian artisans. His most recognizable furniture designs were manufactured by Richardson Nemschoff, as well as a molded fiberglass chair resembling Charles and Ray Eames's famous example.

Vintage advertisement for Lawrence Peabody's designs.

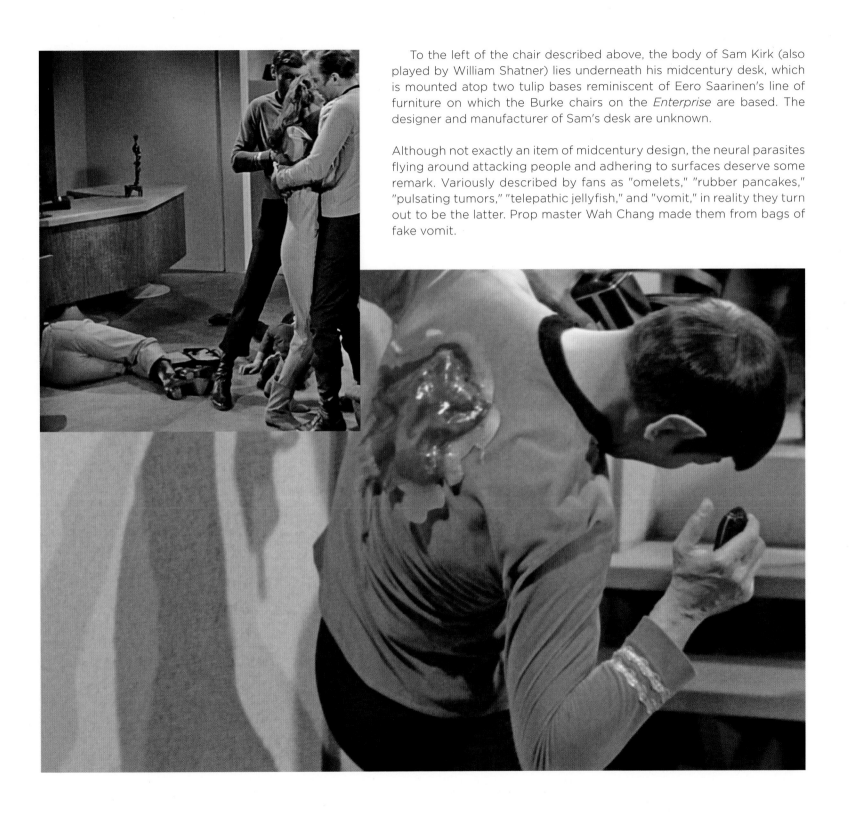

To the left of the chair described above, the body of Sam Kirk (also played by William Shatner) lies underneath his midcentury desk, which is mounted atop two tulip bases reminiscent of Eero Saarinen's line of furniture on which the Burke chairs on the *Enterprise* are based. The designer and manufacturer of Sam's desk are unknown.

Although not exactly an item of midcentury design, the neural parasites flying around attacking people and adhering to surfaces deserve some remark. Variously described by fans as "omelets," "rubber pancakes," "pulsating tumors," "telepathic jellyfish," and "vomit," in reality they turn out to be the latter. Prop master Wah Chang made them from bags of fake vomit.

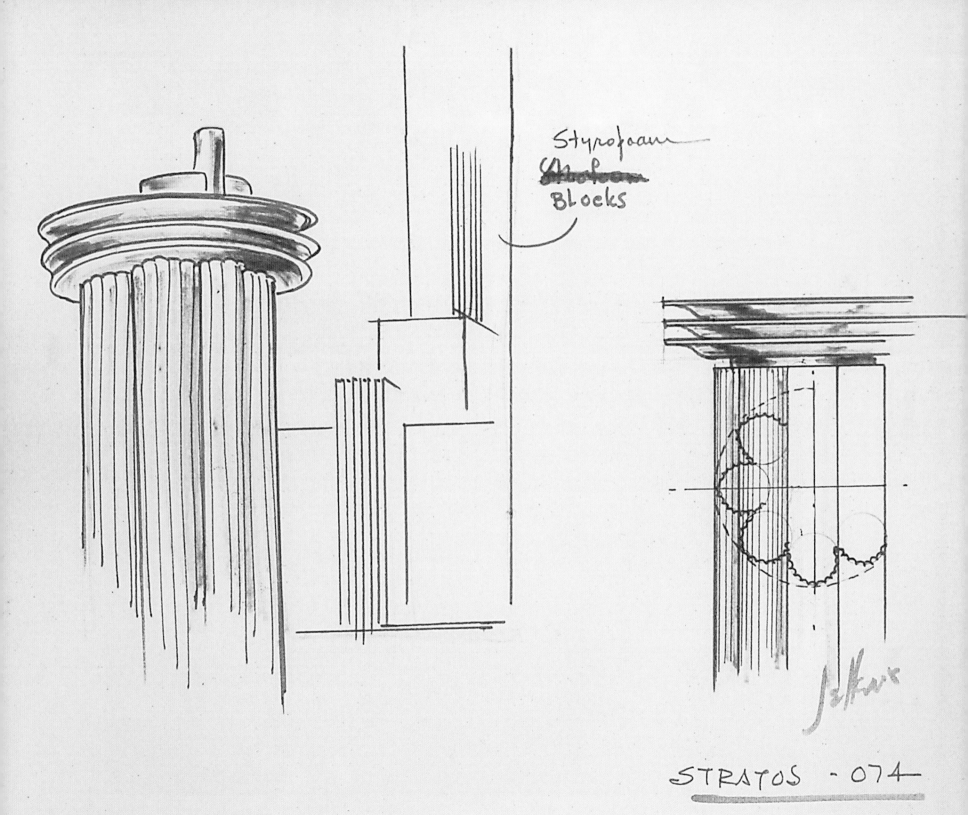

Styrofoam ~~Styrofoam~~ Blocks

STRATOS · 074

FUTURIST ARCHITECTURE

LEFT Matt Jefferies' concept sketch for Stratos in "The Cloud Minders."

The five-year mission for *Star Trek* was to explore strange new worlds and seek out new civilizations. In theory, this meant a new solar system every week. It was a challenge, however, for the production crew to create new and exotic worlds on such a schedule—and on a tight budget. This was especially problematic when entire cityscapes or specific futuristic buildings were needed to convey the plot. Existing studio backlots could be used for shooting only in parallel-universe or time-travel stories such as "Miri," "A Piece of the Action," "The Return of the Archons," and "The City on the Edge of Forever."

To obviate these restrictions, architectural settings were provided in one of three ways: by filming on location using genuine modernist architecture as a backdrop, by building a key structure de novo on a soundstage, or by cinematic cheating—namely, creating the image of the faraway world as a matte painting that could be used as a backdrop onto which live action was superimposed in postproduction. Examples of each of these are given below.

The underground mining station on Janus VI where the *Enterprise* crew encounter the silicon-based Horta creature in "The Devil in the Dark." This painting was used as the establishing shot for the story. Matte painting by Albert Whitlock.

ON-LOCATION SHOOTING

The 110-acre TRW Space and Defense Park in Redondo Beach, California (also known as the Space Park) provided the ideal setting for the world of Deneva as portrayed in "Operation -- Annihilate!" (See discussion of the episode in the Season One chapter). Built between 1960 and 1967, the complex was designed by modernist architect Craig Sturm and landscape architect Arthur Barton, both of Albert C. Martin and Associates (ACMA). The Space Park facility was designed like a college campus, with open green spaces, walkways between buildings, sculptures, and a reflecting pool. ACMA was also responsible for designing Los Angeles's sleek and much-lauded Department of Water and Power Building, built in 1964.

Both photos show TRW Campus in the 1960s.

When the landing party beams down to Deneva, the cityscape—besides being exuberantly futuristic—is eerily empty. The long shots that unfold the breadth of the Space Park reveal spaces empty of people and tend to amplify this feeling of desertion. Only later does the *Enterprise* crew realize that the planet has been invaded by a creature whose individual cells can move independently and thus infect their hosts, hijacking their freedom of will.

Establishing shot of the setting of the landing party's arrival on the planet Deneva, filmed at the TRW facility.

The overhang in the foreground is cleverly used to disguise the TRW logo on the top of the building.

Filmed at the TRW facility.

Schoenberg Hall shortly after completion.

Since 2002, the Space Park facility has been owned by Northrup Grumman and continues today to serve its original purpose of developing missiles, satellites, and space-based technology.

Also featured in the episode "Operation -- Annihilate!" is Schoenberg Hall, the concert hall of the School of Music at UCLA. One of the first modernist buildings on the UCLA campus, it was designed and built in 1954–55 by renowned Los Angeles architect Welton D. Becket, who also designed the Capitol Records Building, Bullocks Pasadena, the Santa Monica Civic Auditorium, the Dorothy Chandler Pavilion and the Mark Taper Forum, and the Cinerama Dome in Century City, as well as numerous office and retail buildings throughout the US. As described by the Los Angeles Conservancy, Schoenberg Hall features simple monumental columns supporting an overhanging roof over a two-story-high glass-walled foyer. Decorating the cornice of the flat roof is a series of mosaic murals designed by C. Richard Haines that depict the history of music. The building's exterior served as the establishing shot representing Sam Kirk's lab on Deneva.

Sam Kirk's laboratory building in "Operation -- Annihilate!"

ZEFRAM COCHRANE'S CABIN

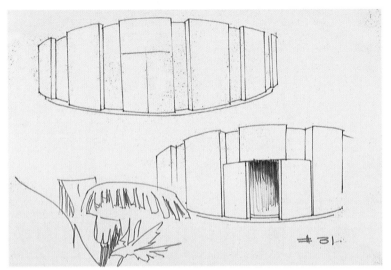

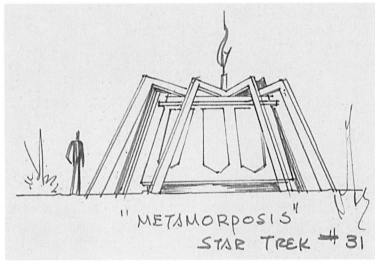

Two early concept drawings by Matt Jefferies for Zefram Cochrane's steel panel cabin.

As a result of a forced landing on an unnamed planetoid, the Enterprise crew encounters a mysterious survivor of the crash: Zefram Cochrane, human inventor of the warp drive. Cochrane's acumen in all things STEM had enabled him to build and furnish for himself a snug all-metal cabin using debris from his vessel. What better way to live for 150 years than in the minimalism of midcentury modern?

The structure used for Cochrane's abode in Season Two's "Metamorphosis" was designed by Matt Jefferies and assembled by the prop department. It featured a hexagonal structure covered by a polygonal roof, clerestory windows, and slightly curved external vertical beams reaching up to support each point of the roof. To the authors' best knowledge, it was never reused in any later episode.

The final modernist cabin sketch by Matt Jefferies and the realized set piece from the episode "Metamorphosis."

The D'Angelo House in Riverside County, California.

Architectural enthusiasts may notice an uncanny resemblance between this structure and the D'Angelo House in the tiny community of Snow Creek in Riverside County, California, which was built in 1963 by the Los Angeles businessman Floyd D'Angelo of the Aluminum Skylight and Specialty Corporation, and aerospace engineer Henry Conrey. The polygonal exterior features alternating triangular aluminum and glass panels, and was designed to slowly rotate on its axis in synchronization with the diurnal movement of the sun. The rotation was powered by an electric motor beneath the house, driving an engaged pinion into a toothed circular rack akin to that of a record turntable.

One might go even further back in the history of architectural design to find the inspiration for Cochrane's cabin: Fritz Lang's 1927 film *Metropolis*, an ominous depiction of the future, that features a towering structure with six expressed projections eerily reminiscent of the points in Cochrane's roof.

From Fritz Lang's 1927 movie *Metropolis*.

MATTE PAINTINGS

Desilu Studios commissioned artist Albert Whitlock (see biography in this chapter) to create a series of matte paintings for both *Star Trek* pilot episodes and several Season One episodes; some of these were reused or reworked for use in subsequent seasons. These paintings variously portrayed Federation colonies, a Starbase, mining and production facilities, and alien civilizations.

The following image illustrates how Matt Jefferies' storyboard for "Errand of Mercy" performed multiple functions. The storyboard provided draft artwork for the matte painting which would provide a backdrop to be added in postproduction. It also showed the set's overall layout, the camera angle on the action, and the small portion of the set that had to be built at Desilu Studios in Culver City for live-action filming. The shot would then be superimposed onto the matte. (See blue outline in image.) Some of Whitlock's matte paintings, such as the Moorish-looking domes on Rigel VII, seem to draw from classical architecture, while others have a Buck Rogers-like feel reminiscent of the Streamline Moderne look of the 1930s. Starbase 11 might have commissioned the modernist architect Ludwig Mies van der Rohe to lend his International style to the high-rise structures. Some fanciful futuristic shapes in these paintings might invoke the Seattle Space Needle, the Los Angeles International Airport's Theme Building, or the Emerald City of Oz.

Owners of the remastered DVD episodes of *Star Trek* may note subtle differences in those matte paintings. Some have been sharpened and enhanced, others recomposed, and still others completely replaced with new artwork by the artist Max Gabl. Those presented herein are from the original unremastered episodes unless otherwise noted.

Whitlock's work conveys an ethereal, dreamlike feel of exotic, faraway places. Each opens and exposes our dreams, just as each offers us a glimpse through a window into a new and different world.

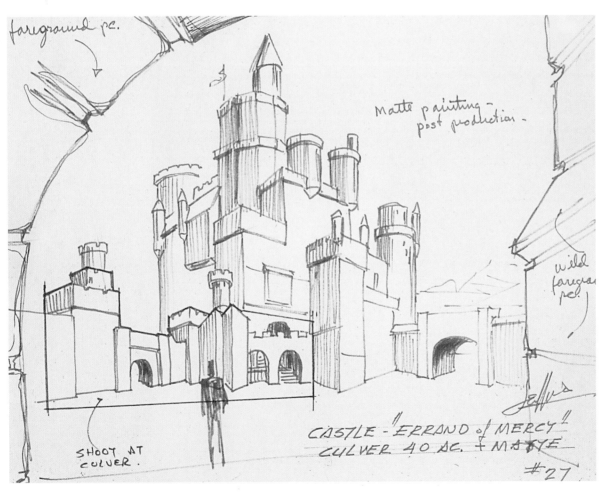

Sketch for set and matte painting for "Errand of Mercy" by Matt Jefferies.

Close-up photo of the original matte painting depicting the citadel on Rigel VII in the first pilot episode "The Cage." Also used as Flint's castle in "A Requiem for Methuselah." Wooden frame is visible on the periphery. Matte painting by Albert Whitlock.

The twenty-third-century city of Mojave, California, appears in the distance beyond Captain Pike and Vina's picnic during a dream sequence in "The Cage." This painting was mounted directly on the set behind the actors. Matte painting by Albert Whitlock.

The view from Dr. Leighton's window on Planet Q in "The Conscience of the King." This appears to be a reutilization of the Mojave matte from "The Cage." Matte painting by Albert Whitlock.

The unmanned dilithium crystal cracking station on Delta Vega, where the *Enterprise* takes Gary Mitchell after his transformation in the second pilot "Where No Man Has Gone Before." This painting was modified and reused as the penal colony on Tantalus V in "Dagger of the Mind." Matte painting by Albert Whitlock.

Starbase 11, the site of Kirk's trial in "Court Martial." Matte painting by Albert Whitlock.

Starbase 11 as it appeared in Parts 1 and 2 of "The Menagerie," where Captain Kirk encounters Captain Pike after his radiation accident. Matte painting by Albert Whitlock.

Portion of the Starbase 11 shot that was filmed in the studio and transposed onto the matte painting.

This crisp, futuristic cityscape belies the devastating 500-year war that the planet Eminiar VII has been waging with its neighbor Vendikar in "A Taste of Armageddon." Image includes portions of the painting not visible in the episode; these were reassembled from original Desilu Studios film clips by Gerald Gurian. Matte painting by Albert Whitlock.

DESIGNING THE CLOUD CITY OF STRATOS

The planet Ardana, as discussed further in the Season Three episode "The Cloud Minders," was a world of contrasts. Troglytes (the ninety-nine-percenters) live on the planet surface and mine zenite, which emits an invisible gas that inhibits mental development. Stratos city dwellers (the one-percenters) live literally in the clouds—a city in the air. Class separation is made possible by a strictly enforced social structure and by the wonders of antigravity, as Stratos floats high in the sky, out of the Troglytes' reach.

To bring this dreamlike city to life, Matt Jefferies first drew a series of storyboards and concept drawings of the city itself and the various spaces that had to be built to portray Stratos. Some of these drawings guided the matte painting; others informed the set design and decoration.

In the plans for the matte painting of the city, one can trace how the drawings move from the general to the specific as first the form and then the actual shapes materialize. Two final matte paintings are also presented: the original as painted by Albert Whitlock and the painting used in the remastered DVDs that show a city reimagined by artist Max Gabl. Both invoke the atmosphere necessary to convey the storyline, and both appear true to the original concept of Matt Jefferies.

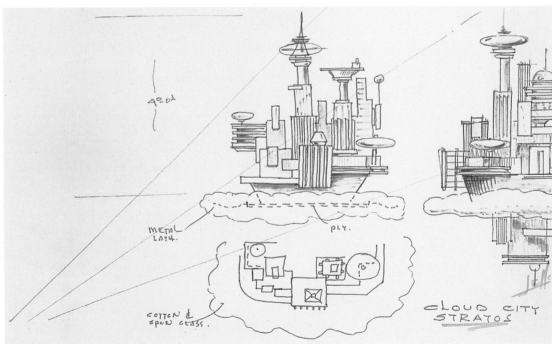

Two concept drawings by Matt Jefferies for the Cloud City of Stratos.

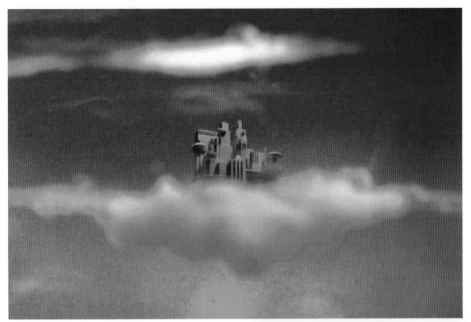

Original matte painting by Albert Whitlock

Notable in the aesthetic of the cloud city of Stratos is a style we Earthers term Brutalism, defined by its blocklike architectural structures, raw exposed concrete, and, in art, harsh textures and jagged edges—paradoxical for a city of serenity and reflection. This is discussed in more detail in the Brutalism chapter.

The remastered matte painting by Max Gabl.

The following images compare Matt Jefferies' original concept sketch with the ultimate set as built and furnished by the set designers and decorators. Some sketches by Jefferies for "The Cloud Minders" were never realized, while others were modified or simplified—presumably to contain costs.

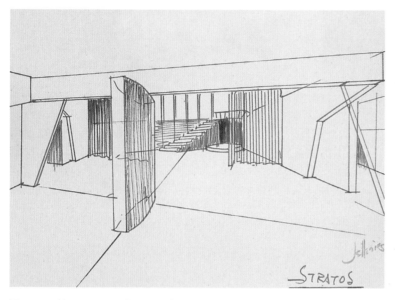

The reception area on Stratos where visitors materialize.

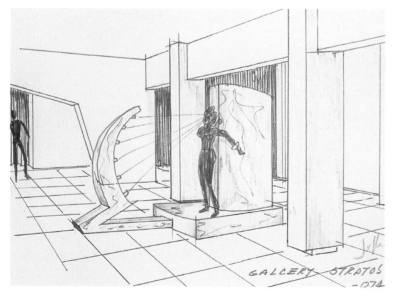

The torture chamber where Vanna (Charlene Polite) was interrogated.

The detention cell where Vanna was held.

MATTE ARTIST

ALBERT WHITLOCK, an artist in the film industry, was born in Britain in 1915. His career in film began at Gaumont Studios in London, where he worked first as a page, then a set builder, and later as a grip. He performed miniature and painting work for Alfred Hitchcock in the 1930s on *The Man Who Knew Too Much* and *The 39 Steps*.

Whitlock began doing matte painting during the 1940s and was recruited by Walt Disney in the 1950s, at which time he moved to the United States. He worked for Disney Studios for seven years, doing both film work and design work on Disneyland. He moved to Universal Studios in 1961, serving as the head of the matte department. Desilu Studios tapped Whitlock's talent during the mid-1960s, for which he provided several matte paintings for both pilot episodes of *Star Trek*: "The Cage," and "Where No Man Has Gone Before," as well as several subsequent episodes in Season One. Some of these paintings were recycled or reworked for use in episodes of the subsequent seasons.

Following *Star Trek*, he created over 70 matte paintings for the movie *Earthquake* in 1974, for which he won an Academy Award. Other films to which he contributed include *The Hindenburg, Greystoke: The Legend of Tarzan, Dune, Mame, Bound for Glory, The Thing,* and *High Anxiety.*

Whitlock retired in 1985 and died in Santa Barbara in 1999.

SEASON TWO

 METAMORPHOSIS

Season 2 • **Production Sequence** 31 • **Air Date** November 10, 1967 • **Stardate** 3219.8
Art Director Rolland M. Brooks, Walter M. "Matt" Jefferies • **Set Decorator** Joseph J. Stone • **Property Master** Irving A. Feinberg

SYNOPSIS

Captain Kirk, Mr. Spock, and Dr. McCoy are escorting Commissioner Nancy Hedford (Elinor Donahue from *Father Knows Best*) to the *Enterprise* for vital medical treatment when the shuttlecraft is waylaid by a cloud-like creature and compelled to land on a small planetoid. There they meet a virile young human castaway who purports to be Zefram Cochrane (Glenn Corbett), who disappeared 150 years ago as an elderly man.

It turns out that he has developed a creepy symbiotic relationship with a sentient force field he calls the Companion, who had healed Cochrane and is keeping him young. The Companion has

fetched the *Enterprise* personnel to relieve his boredom and now won't let them leave. Ultimately, the Companion merges with the dying commissioner, healing her, and Zefram and Nancy decide to remain on the planet together.

Star Trek fans will note that the episode airing immediately after this one, "Journey to Babel," featured Jane Wyatt (as Spock's human mother, Amanda Grayson), another veteran actor from *Father Knows Best* who portrayed Elinor Donahue's mother in that classic TV show.

"Yes, I had tools and supplies left over from my crash—not Earth, of course, but it's livable."

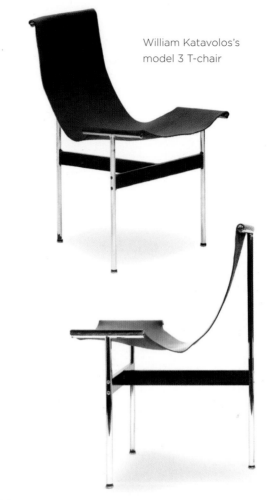

William Katavolos's model 3 T-chair

▶ T-CHAIR FOR LAVERNE · USA · 1952
DESIGNERS: WILLIAM KATAVOLOS, DOUGLAS KELLEY, AND ROSS LITTELL

Entering Cochrane's cabin, the *Enterprise* crew are struck by the elegant and trendy furnishings of one who claims to be a shipwreck survivor. In building everything from scratch, Cochrane was apparently channeling some well-known mid-twentieth-century designers. In the foreground of the picture below is the iconic T-Chair by William Katavolos.

Katavolos, a New York City–born architect, furniture designer, sculptor, and educator, received his bachelor's degree in industrial design at Pratt institute in 1949. He was awarded a first prize in furniture design by the Museum of Modern Art (MoMA) in New York in 1952–53, and by the American Institute Design in 1953–54. Katavolos is also an accomplished sculptor, having exhibited his work worldwide and taught at the Pratt Institute for over forty years.

Katavolos designed furniture lines for several companies, including George Nelson Associates, Frankel/Robert John, and Laverne International. It was for Laverne International that Katavolos teamed up with designers Douglas Kelley and Ross Littell to design the T-Chair model 3LC for its New Furniture series. The T-Chair is in MoMA's permanent collection.

The leather sling of the chair almost appears to float. Three steel T-rod legs act as the structural base of the chair. Sculptural and minimalist in its design, the T-Chair was a radical design for the decade in which it was designed—the 1950s. The chair is a harmonious union of vertical and horizontal planes.

On the right side of the living area in the image above is a black modernist club chair and matching side table of an unidentified designer. Although similar to a design by the Danish designer Poul Nørreklit for the manufacturer Hovedstadens Møbelfabrik, subtle differences preclude a definitive assignment.

Besides looking great for his age, Zefram Cochrane was one smart dude. In addition to being the inventor of warp drive, he hand-built his all-metal modernist cabin and the trendy furniture and artwork within using the debris from his crashed vessel! His metal cabin is discussed further in the "Futurist Architecture" chapter.

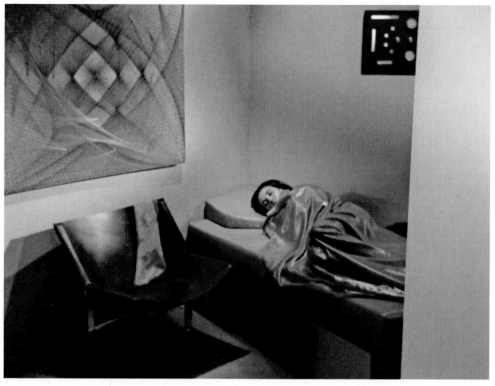

▶ MODEL 248 CHAIR FOR LEIF WESSMAN ASSOCIATES INC. · USA · 1963
DESIGNER: CLEMENT MEADMORE

In the sleeping area within Cochrane's home, Nancy Hedford lies fever-ish. Next to the bed where she rests sits a single chair designed by Clement Meadmore.

Meadmore was an Australian sculptor, designer, and author who studied at the Melbourne Institute of Technology, where he focused on aeronautical engineering and industrial design. He is mostly known for his massively bold and minimalist sculptures in bronze and steel. Mead-more was greatly Influenced by the abstract expressionist movement in 1950s New York, and the painter Barnett Newman, as well as jazz music. He is the author of several books, among them *How to Make Furniture Without Tools,* and *The Modern Chair: Classic Designs by Thonet, Breuer, Le Corbusier, Eames, and Others.*

Little is known about the design of the model 248 chair itself. The leather seat of the deceptively simple-looking chair floats seamlessly atop an H-shape chrome base. The ergonomic furnishing looks like it could have been mindfully and elegantly made from salvaged spaceship parts, with its two screws holding the leather seat tightly in place. Like Katavolos's T-chair, this chair is in MoMA's permanent collection.

▶ STRING ART · 1960s

Above the Clement Meadmore chair in the photograph on the previous page hangs a large wall piece made of brightly colored thread strung together to form a geometric pattern that contrasts sharply with the amorphous shape of the Companion. String art became a fashionable trend in the 1960s and was readily available through books and how-to kits (including for *Star Trek* string art, no less!). Its origins date back to mathematician Mary Everest Boole in the nineteenth century as a means of making mathematical ideas understandable to children. The string art in Cochrane's home is in complete harmony with his geometric and austere furnishings throughout and is a perfect pastime for castaways with time on their hands.

Also visible in the living area on the wall are two metal wall sculptures that Cochrane ostensibly constructed using scraps of salvaged metal. These and other designs are discussed further in the "Brutalism" chapter.

"All the comforts of home, indeed, Mr. Cochrane. Where'd you get the antiques?"

Dwyer later in life.

JOHN DWYER, set decorator on *Star Trek*, was born in Detroit in 1935. "I was a Hollywood brat from the word *go*," Dwyer said about his career in the film industry during a 2017 interview with author Dan Chavkin. Dwyer's father was a prop man at MGM Studios, and his grandfather also worked in the film industry. Dwyer graduated from Marshall High School in the Los Feliz district of Los Angeles, and rejected a basketball scholarship from UCLA in order to enlist in the navy, serving during the Korean War.

After serving in the navy for four years, Dwyer began night classes at age 23, at the Chouinard Art Institute in Los Angeles. It was Dwyer's father who eventually got him a job at Universal Studios in Burbank and into the union as a set decorator.

Dwyer's active career spanned five decades. His first job was on the television show *River Boat* (1959-61), starring a young Burt Reynolds. Prior to *Star Trek*, Dwyer worked on the TV series' *McHale's Navy* (1966), *Mr. Terrific* (1967), and the westerns *Laredo* (1966–67) and *The Virginian* (1966–67)—all for Universal Studios.

It was during Season Two, for the episode "The Trouble with Tribbles," that Dwyer's *Star Trek* career began. Responsible for acquiring the appropriate props and dressing the set, he visited stores throughout the Los Angeles area looking for just the right pieces to populate the sets for each episode. Because of his previous work at Universal Studios, Dwyer was allowed to access its prop department on behalf of *Star Trek*.

In an interview for the special feature "Designing the Final Frontier" for the remastered DVDs for the series, Dwyer described his work: "The art director . . . supplies all of the hard things that you see. Then I would come in and do carpeting, drapery treatments, all of the furniture and wall designs, decorations, and pretty much put everything together. . . . We had to be really inventive; we didn't have any money." Because of his $500-per-episode budget, Dwyer became known for improvising: reusing discarded set materials and scrounging through Dumpsters to reuse packing materials and other trash.

Besides his work on 38 episodes of *TOS*, his contribution spans several iterations of the franchise, including 25 episodes of *Star Trek: The Next Generation*, the feature films *Star Trek IV: The Voyage Home*, *Star Trek V: The Final Frontier*, *Star Trek: Generations*, *Star Trek: First Contact*, *Star Trek: Insurrection*, and *Star Trek: Nemesis*.

Notable other work included set decoration on *The Young Lawyers*, *Night Gallery*, *Dragnet*, *Kojak*, *Columbo*, *Ellery Queen*, *Centennial*, *Magnum PI*, *MacGyver*, and numerous feature movies including *Jaws*, *Coalminer's Daughter*, *Beverly Hills Cop*, *Thief*, *The Thing*, and *Terminator II*. Dwyer received an Academy Award nomination for *Coal Miner's Daughter*, an Emmy nomination for *Centennial*, and he won an Emmy for art direction for the series *Gangster Chronicles*.

Dwyer was a founding member of the Set Decorators Society of America, and received their Lifetime Achievement Award in 2012. After more than 40 years in the industry, he retired in 2002 to Encinitas, California, where he died in 2018.

A youthful John Dwyer on the set of Season Three's "That Which Survives."

THE TROUBLE WITH TRIBBLES

Season 2 • **Production Sequence** 42 • **Air Date** December 29, 1967 • **Stardate** 4523.3
Art Director Walter M. "Matt" Jefferies • **Set Decorator** John M. Dwyer • **Property Master** Irving A. Feinberg

SYNOPSIS

Space Station K-7 becomes the focal point of sabotage, intrigue, and intragalactic rivalry centering around quadrotriticale, a four-lobed hybrid of wheat and rye that is key to the Federation's successful development of the contested Sherman's Planet. Lieutenant Uhura unwittingly jeopardizes all with her acquisition of a tribble, a purring, furry ball of relentless reproductive capacity—and an appetite for quadrotriticale. William Campbell plays Koloth, the duplicitious, conniving Klingon commander who delights in pushing Captain Kirk's buttons. Viewers will also recognize Patty Duke's stage father William Schallert, who plays the officious undersecretary in charge of agricultural affairs for the Federation, who also serves to amplify Kirk's headaches.

This episode, with the first TV script written by now-noted science fiction author David Gerrold, was nominated for a Hugo Award in 1968 and is perhaps the best known and best loved of all *Star Trek* episodes.

▶ ORIGAMI CHAIR FOR ST. JOHN SEATING CORP. · USA · 1960

DESIGNER: PAUL MCCOBB

When the Klingons on shore leave start spewing disparaging remarks about the *Enterprise*, a Wild West–like barroom brawl ensues between the respective crewmen amid several midcentury Origami chairs. Because the filming of the K-7 lounge scene required twenty-four matching chairs, set decorator John Dwyer had to pull them off show-room floors from all over Los Angeles County. According to David Gerrold, the script writer for "The Trouble with Tribbles," who was present for the shooting, the tricky fight sequence had to be care-fully choreographed so that the borrowed Origami chairs were not at risk of damage. The tables built by Dwyer for the scene, however, were fair game for mistreatment.

Paul McCobb's influence on midcentury modern design cannot be overstated. McCobb designed for such diverse furniture groups as Planner, Perimeter, Delinea-tor, Linear, and Predictor, and his designs exemplified a new kind of minimalism in postwar America. Both a designer and a decorator, McCobb estab-lished his own design firm in 1945 with partner B.G. Mes-berg, and launched the Plan-ner Group and Directional furniture lines. Other prod-ucts he designed included radios, televisions, and hi-fi consoles.

McCobb also went on to design for other furniture companies, including Calvin, Irvin, and H. Sacks and Sons, as well as the St. John Seat-ing Corporation, for whom he designed the Origami chair. This piece was McCobb's foray into the affordable material of molded plastic and was offered in an armrest-equipped version on several configurations of metal bases. The angularity of the chairs recalls the delicate shapes of folded paper—hence the name *Origami*.

"I meant to say that the *Enterprise* should be hauled away *as* garbage."

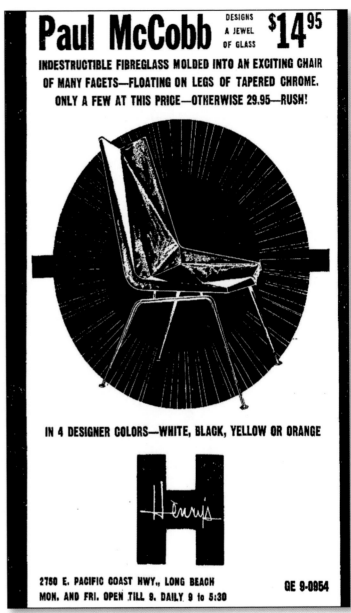

LEFT A trio of Paul McCobb's faceted Origami chairs. ABOVE Vintage advertisement of Henry's furniture store in Long Beach for McCobb's Origami chairs.

"The whah-what? What's quadrotriticale—wheat, so what?"

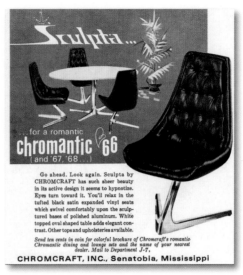

Advertisement from 1966 for the Chromcraft Sculpta chair.

Chromcraft's sleek Sculpta chair.

▶ 'SCULPTA' CHAIR FOR CHROMCRAFT · USA · 1966

Upon arriving at Space Station K-7, Captain Kirk and Mr. Spock are met by station manager Lurry (Whit Bissell), Undersecretary Nilz Baris (William Schallert), and two Klingons demanding shore leave privileges. A solitary chair is all that separates Kirk from the Klingon captain, Koloth.

"Go ahead. Look again. Sculpta by CHROMCRAFT has such sheer beauty in its active design it seems to hypnotize," reads the 1966 advertisement for the Sculpta chair. Chromcraft is a Mississippi-based furniture company that specializes in swivel-tilt casters. The Sculpta chair has a quilted vinyl seat cantilevered over a solid-cast polished aluminum V-shaped base. The futuristic-looking chevron shape seems to propel the chair forward.

This distinctive base appears to be inspired by German-born visionary designer Vladimir Kagan, closely matching his Unicorn sofa from 1963. Emigrating to the United States as a child, Kagan learned to make furniture by working with his father, a master cabinetmaker. A student of architecture at New York's School of Industrial Art and Columbia University, Kagan opened his own shop in 1948 and became the toast of celebrities and wealthy clientele alike. With his use of curvaceous forms on sculptural bases, his furniture designs were atypical of the minimalist midcentury modern aesthetic of the day; each piece was a stand-alone work of functional art. Often copied and rarely matched, Kagan went on to design the lounge at the United Nations in New York and received commissions from General Electric, Walt Disney, General Motors, and Monsanto.

⊀ASSIGNMENT: EARTH

Season 2 • **Production Sequence** 55 • **Air Date** March 29, 1968 • **Stardate** Unknown
Art Director Walter "Matt" Jefferies • **Set Decorator** John Dwyer • **Property Masters** Irving A. Feinberg

SYNOPSIS

This was an unusual episode that represented a spin-off pilot for a series that, so to speak, never left the launchpad. Using the "light speed breakaway factor" (a newly acquired technique for time travel), the crew of the *Enterprise* travel back to the twentieth century and encounter mysterious intergalactic secret agent Gary Seven and his clueless earth secretary Roberta Lincoln (Robert Lansing and Teri Garr, respectively). The setting: the eve of a critical event in the balance of global powers involving the launch of a sub-warhead platform by the US that risks going awry. This time-travel story poses a difficult dilemma: By intervening in history, did the *Enterprise* crew risk changing the future, or were they acting to ensure the correct outcome?

Irrespective, what better way to study midcentury design than to go back to mid-twentieth-century Earth? The Manhattan office of Gary Seven is slickly decorated with a plethora of mid-century modern pieces. We are also treated to views of the command headquarters of Kennedy Space Center one year before the US moon launch and landing, complete with ground engineers in white shirts and pocket protectors.

Earth. 1968. Mid-twentieth-century Manhattan. Gary Seven enters his executive office that is filled with a collection of midcentury modern furnishings fit for a top-secret agent. Opposite a unique desk are two plush, handsomely tufted club chairs in the style of Dorothy Draper, as well as the equally plush sofa situated behind them. Between the chairs is an octagonal coffee table by RS Associates, whose geometric shape echoes pure modernism. A simple but elegant hanging lamp of an unidentified designer is seen, along with an assortment of abstract paintings and sculptures throughout this very sophisticated office.

▶ BOOMERANG EXECUTIVE DESK T-SERIES FOR TECNO · ITALY · 1954

DESIGNER: OSVALDO BORSANI

Gary Seven's executive desk, attributed to Osvaldo Borsani, is not your standard boss's desk. The desktop seems to float atop two swivel drawer units.

Born in 1911 in Varedo Switzerland, Borsani studied architecture at the Politecnico di Milan, graduating in 1936. His father, Gaetano, was a well-known furniture maker. While still a student, Borsani designed the Casa Minima project for the Milan Triennale, earning him a silver medal award. In 1943, he designed and built his own house, the Villa Borsani, in Varedo. Upon graduating, Borsani joined the family business, Atelier Varedo, as a furniture designer. In 1953, he established the firm Tecno with his brother Fulgenzio. The firm was known for modern technology advancements in furniture design. Besides manufacturing Borsani's designs, the firm introduced furniture by designers Gio Ponti, Gae Aulenti and Carlo de Carli. Borsani's work for Tecno can be found in the permanent collections of MoMA, the Victoria and Albert Museum in London, and the Triennale di Milano in Italy.

▶ EXPO '67 SIDE TABLES BY RS ASSOCIATES LTD. OF MONTREAL · CANADA · 1967

Originally designed expressly for the Canada Pavilion at Expo '67 in Montreal, this octagonal side table appeared on display along with an entire line of furniture. Coffee tables, side tables, vanities, desks, and dressers were among the pieces designed for the exposition, held in Montreal from April 27–October 29, 1967. With sixty-two nations participating, it was considered one of the most successful world's fairs. The following year, the Expo '67 furniture line was offered to the public by RS Associates.

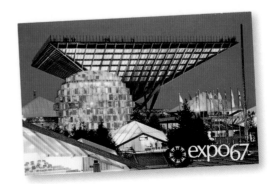

▶ HOLLYWOOD REGENCY TUFTED BUCKET SWIVEL CHAIRS AND COUCH · USA · 1960s
DESIGNER: ATTRIBUTED TO DOROTHY DRAPER

The Hollywood Regency style, or Regency Moderne, is described as being ornate, extravagant, and bold in design and was inspired by the stately and glamorous homes of actors and actresses in Hollywood from the 1920s to the 1950s. The movement is said to have been spawned by famous American interior decorator Doro- thy Draper, whose flair for home interior design extended to hotels such as the Sherry-Netherland Hotel in New York and the Fairmont in San Francisco. This design style, originally referred to as Modern Baroque, was considered by some to be the antithesis of cleaner and simpler modernism.

▶ MR. CHAIR FOR PLYCRAFT INC. · USA · 1960s
DESIGNER: GEORGE MULHAUSER

Fleetingly visible in the outer waiting room is a George Mulhauser–designed "Mr. Chair." Above the chair is a modernist wall-mounted light fixture of unknown make.

Mulhauser, a furniture designer, got his start as a member of the George Nelson Associates design team. It was there that he designed the iconic Coconut chair (1955) for George Nelson. In 1953, he became one of the first recipients of the Pratt Institute's design degree. Mulhauser was then hired by Plycraft founder Paul Goldman, for whom he designed a line called Mr. Chair: the first reclining chair made from a single sheet of plywood, which he created in his home studio. Other iterations of the chair soon followed: There was even a Mrs. Chair. He also designed for the company Directional Industries.

Famous Names in Design

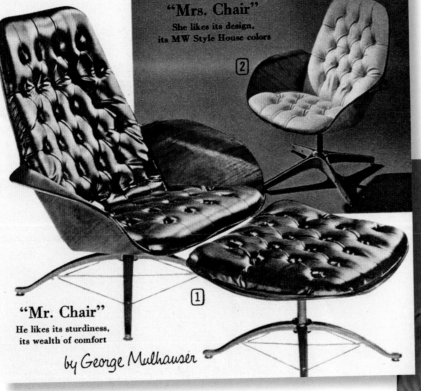

Style House APPROVED SELECTIONS

[1] "MR. CHAIR" by George Mulhauser. Swivel Chair and Ottoman. Foam-cushioned, tufted upholstery of heavy-weight, Leather-grain supported U.S. Naugahyde Plastic. Genuine Walnut, molded plywood frame, solid Walnut legs; Brass-toned steel rods. 38x36x34½ in. high. Ottoman: 21½x25x14 in. high. *Upholstery in Black, White or Tan.*
66 A 2152R–Chair and Ottoman. Ship. wt. 70 lbs. $9.50 Month. *State color.* Cash **$179.95**
66 A 2151R–Chair Only. Ship. wt. 50 lbs. $7.50 Month. *State color* . . . . . . Cash   139.95

[2] "MRS. CHAIR." No Ottoman. Like "Mr. Chair" but steel-reinforced Walnut base. 26x26 in. wide, 32½ in. high. *State upholstery Color:* MW* Capri Blue, Coin Gold; also Black. No Money Down on Easy Terms.
66 A 2153 R—Abt. 28¾x23x32½ in. high overall. Ship. wt. 40 lbs. $5 Month. Cash **$94.95**

"Mrs. Chair"
She likes its design,
its MW Style House colors

"Mr. Chair"
He likes its sturdiness,
its wealth of comfort

by George Mulhauser

Vintage advertisement for the Mr. Chair and Mrs. Chair.

"WHAT I WILL TAKE CREDIT FOR IS, I SURROUNDED MYSELF BY VERY BRIGHT PEOPLE WHO CAME UP WITH ALL THOSE WONDERFUL THINGS. AND THEN YOU CAN APPEAR VERY SMART."

—GENE RODDENBERRY

Closer view of the unidentified sconce between Mr. Spock and Captain Kirk.

▶ GOODFORM ADJUSTABLE ALUMINUM CHAIR MODEL 2123 BY GENERAL FIREPROOFING COMPANY · USA · 1932

Gary Seven carries out his covert mission of sabotage at the McKinley Rocket Base (a fictitious location; Kennedy Space Center was used for the establishing shots). The launch control room features model 2123 Goodform chairs for the team of scientists.

Goodform is the name of the seating line introduced in 1932 by the General Fireproofing Company. The company was founded in 1902 in Youngstown, Ohio, as a manufacturer of building materials. Office furniture was first produced by the company in 1907. The company's first steel desk was introduced in 1923. Although the world's first all-aluminum office chair was produced by Alcoa in 1924, the all-aluminum Goodform model 2123 was released in 1932. Over the next seven years, ten models were produced.

Speaking of office furniture, Gary Seven's Manhattan office is equipped with the latest Royal Emperor Electric Typewriter. Designed by George H. Kress for the Royal McBee Corporation and introduced circa 1965, this bad boy features the Magic Monitor, the Magic Meter, and the Magic Margin—not to mention Royal Touch Control. And it came in a variety of "executive-suite decor" colors.

Finally, this episode provides an interesting example of how Matt Jefferies' concept drawings were ultimately translated into the final set for filming. The accompanying images show Jefferies' vision of Gary Seven's office with the bookcase that rotates to reveal his control center, as well as a photograph from the episode. Note how closely the camera angle for this shot corresponds with Jefferies' original specification, with a desk surface visible in the left foreground and a modernist chair in the background.

Mid-1960s advertisement for the Royal Electress typewriter, similar in styling to the Emperor.

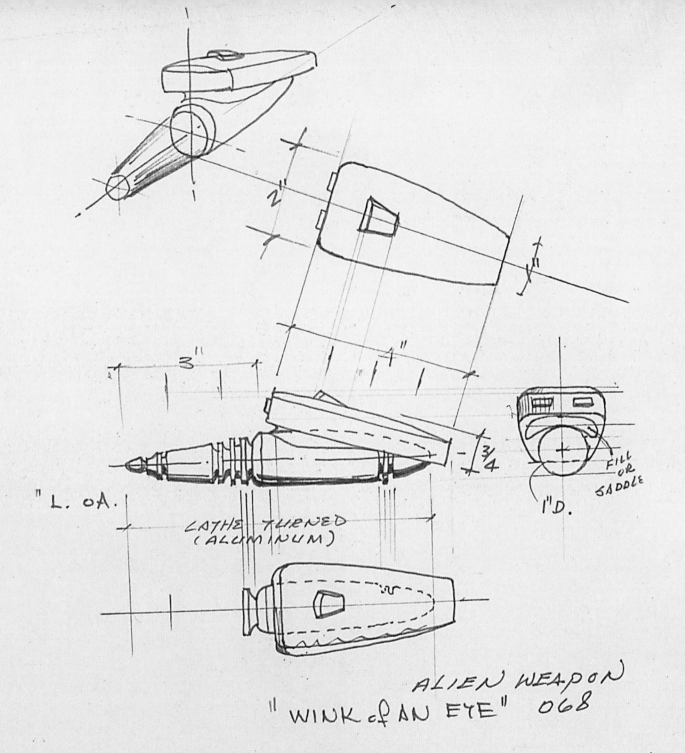

2"

1"

3"

3/4

"L. OA.

LATHE TURNED
(ALUMINUM)

1"D.

FILL
OR
SADDLE

ALIEN WEAPON
"WINK of AN EYE" 068

Jefferies

SET DECORATION, PROPS, AND FASHION

LEFT Matt Jefferies' sketches for implements used in "Wink of an Eye."

In addition to the wealth of midcentury modern furniture found in key episodes featured in this book, we noticed numerous miscellaneous objects in other episodes throughout the three seasons of *Star Trek* that we could not ignore, and that are presented in this chapter.

Certain props are actually everyday items of the 1960s repurposed for the twenty-third century. The many examples of metal screens or decorative grilles that served structural, architectural, and dramatic roles in the show warrant mention. We offer a peek into the personal quarters of certain crew members to see how they live and what they collect. Finally, we examine how the overall futuristic "look" of the *U.S.S. Enterprise* influenced fashion in the late 1960s.

Publicity still showing the vast expanse of the Enterprise's impulse engines through the hexagonal metal grille in engineering.

THE SUPER 8MM MOVIE CAMERA

In the Season Two episode "Patterns of Force," consequences of violating the Prime Directive on the planet Ekos become shockingly clear. Cultural contamination had resulted when Federation history professor John Gill created an authoritarian regime in the image of twentieth-century Nazi Germany. Kirk and Mr. Spock aid the resistance movement and, in order to confront Gill, penetrate headquarters by impersonating Nazi officers filming a VIP. As part of their ploy, they use a Nizo Super 8mm Cine Film camera made by Braun AG.

Oberheim made his debut designing the Nizo Super 8mm camera, which was introduced in 1965. It was a significant advance for Braun's photo division, which, beginning with portable flash units, expanded to 35mm film cameras, slide and film projectors, film splicers, and the Nizo Super 8 Cine Film Camera. Highly ergonomic and minimalist in design, the aluminum-body Nizo camera set the standard for the amateur film market. The camera debuted in New York just one year after the Braun/Chemex Corporation exhibition at MoMA. The camera was also innovative in its use of Super 8 cassettes in place of spooled film. Mainly known for the Super 8 camera, Oberheim also designed kitchen appliances, slide projectors, oral-care products, hair dryers, and shavers for Braun.

From "Patterns of Force."

German industrial designer Robert Oberheim studied at the School of Applied Arts in Wiesbaden, Germany. He designed for Braun between 1960 and 1994 under the direction of legendary design director Dieter Rams. In 1973, Oberheim became deputy director of design at Braun, working alongside designers Hans Gugelot, Dietrich Lubs, Reinhold Weiss, and Peter Hartwein.

Vintage Braun advertisement for the Nizo Super 8mm camera.

SAURIAN BRANDY DECANTER

Mr. Scott couldn't get enough of it. Kirk's alter ego staggered through the *Enterprise* corridors, swigging it on his way to Yeoman Rand's cabin. Even Dr. McCoy, in rare moments, would moderately indulge in it. One of the most ubiquitous props throughout the three seasons of *TOS* is the distinctive curved-neck decanter holding the most popular delicacy in the galaxy: Saurian brandy.

The powderhorn decanter was a product of the George Dickel Brewery in Tennessee and actually was made to hold whisky—or to be more precise, sour mash Tennessee whiskey. This amber-colored bottle, with a leather yoke or harness for easy toting, was sold throughout the 1960s. It was an obvious choice for a twenty-third-century decanter.

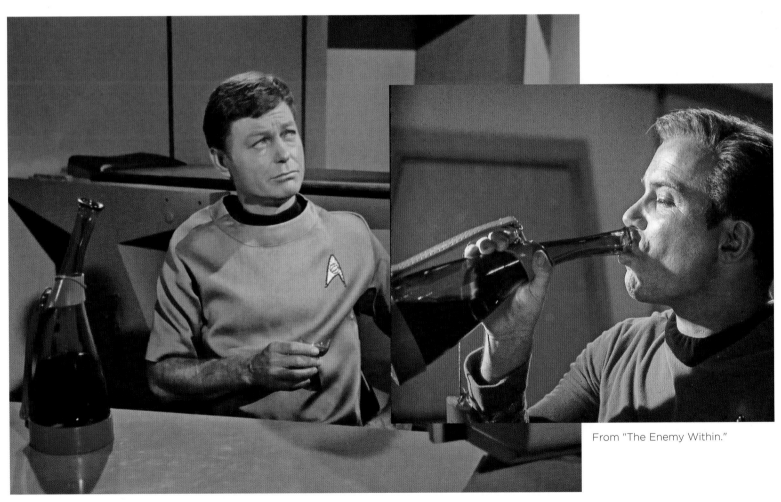

From "The Enemy Within."

And please, Mr. Spock, if you won't join me, don't disapprove of me—at least until you've tried it."
From "The Conscience of the King."

Give 'em the Dickel

Dickel is the whisky that made bottle gifts respectable. Dickel is that fine, old, Charcoal-Gentled Tennessee Sour Mash Whisky—as perfected by George Dickel. It's the whisky that takes the long, slow, *extra* step of Charcoal-Gentling to *smooth* the flavor. And, George Dickel is the only whisky to put itself into these personalized *year-round* gift bottles: the Golf Trophy quart for the sportsman, the leatherbound Powderhorn Decanter—a long-lived conversation piece—and the familiar bottle in holiday wrap for the traditionalist. This holiday season, let yourself go . . . and give 'em the Dickel. In fact give 'em the Dickel any time and make any season a holiday.

Geo. A. Dickel & Co., 90 Proof, Tullahoma, Tennessee

A George Dickel whisky decanter with original box.

"Give 'em the Dickel," indeed.

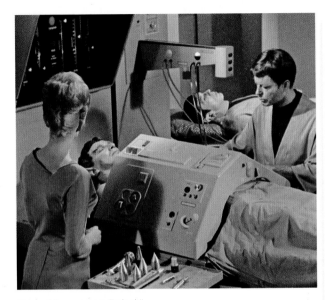

From "Journey to Babel."

The salt and pepper shakers originally chosen for the salt-vampire story in "The Man Trap" were aluminum with a conical shape like miniature space capsules. These were deemed too futuristic, with only a tenuous resemblance to salt and pepper shakers, and hence were replaced with the clear-glass Wilhelm Wagenfeld shakers for that episode.

However, the first set of shakers made numerous appearances in later episodes, playing a variety of roles. Most frequently, they functioned as surgical scalpels. According to the *Star Trek Star Fleet Technical Manual*, the devices provide a surgical cutting width of one, two, or three angstrom units, depending upon the model.[1] In "Journey to Babel," Dr. McCoy employs these instruments when Mr. Spock's father, Ambassador Sarek, requires emergency cardiac surgery. These utensils can also be spotted in Dr. McCoy's sickbay in numerous other episodes.

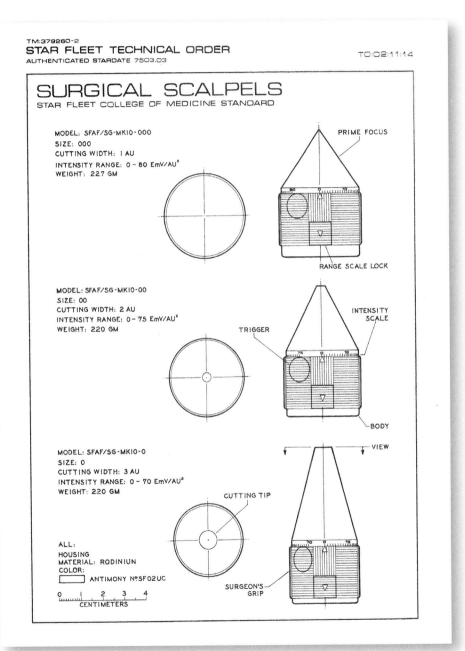

TM:379260-2
STAR FLEET TECHNICAL ORDER
AUTHENTICATED STARDATE 7503.03

TO:02:11:14

SURGICAL SCALPELS
STAR FLEET COLLEGE OF MEDICINE STANDARD

MODEL: SFAF/SG-MKIO-000
SIZE: 000
CUTTING WIDTH: I AU
INTENSITY RANGE: 0 – 80 EmV/AU²
WEIGHT: 227 GM

PRIME FOCUS

RANGE SCALE LOCK

MODEL: SFAF/SG-MKIO-00
SIZE: 00
CUTTING WIDTH: 2 AU
INTENSITY RANGE: 0 – 75 EmV/AU²
WEIGHT: 220 GM

INTENSITY SCALE

TRIGGER

BODY

MODEL: SFAF/SG-MKIO-0
SIZE: 0
CUTTING WIDTH: 3 AU
INTENSITY RANGE: 0 – 70 EmV/AU²
WEIGHT: 220 GM

VIEW

CUTTING TIP

ALL:
HOUSING
MATERIAL: RODINIUN
COLOR:
ANTIMONY №SF02UC

SURGEON'S GRIP

0 1 2 3 4
CENTIMETERS

From the *Star Trek Star Fleet Technical Manual* by Franz Joseph.

Similar but not identical to the Stelton shakers, these conical devices were used to build androids in "Return to Tomorrow," costarring actress Diana Muldaur.

In "Return to Tomorrow," similar shakers perform an indeterminate function in the construction of androids by Sargon and Thalassa (in the bodies of Captain Kirk and Dr. Anne Mulhall, respectively) that eventually were to hold their essences. Since, in a surgical, context the devices could both cut and fuse tissue, perhaps these were used rather like futuristic soldering irons in sealing circuitry connections.

In our world, these are Danish Modern salt and pepper shakers made of chrome and teak. These were part of the Kitchen Line of products from Stelton Denmark, a company created by, and named after, two army buddies: Niels Stellan Hom and Carton Medelaire. The two began producing stainless steel products through the company Danish Stainless during the 1960s. The company was also known for making and marketing a line of stainless home goods created by the famous designer and architect Arne Jacobsen.

Stelton shaker.

ROOM DIVIDERS AND DECORATIVE GRILLES

Throughout the *Enterprise,* and on numerous other special sets, decorative screens or metal grilles serve a variety of functions. Some, such as those in the crews' quarters, are used as room dividers that separate an open space into distinct living areas. Metal grilles are also seen in engineering that allow unobstructed views of equipment and engine machinery.

Brise-soleil (from the French term for "sun breaker") are the outdoor twentieth-century counterparts to these indoor decorative screens. These were used in midcentury construction, particularly in the rapidly growing communities of the southwestern US. Besides their use in blocking sunlight, they were employed for privacy in front of large glass windows, to screen off unsightly elements such as air conditioning units or utility meters, to enclose patios, and for mere ornamentation. Architect Edward Durell Stone is perhaps best known for popularizing this building material, and many examples are extant today, particularly in desert resorts such as Palm Springs.[2]

Decorative screens for internal use also became popular in the mid-twentieth century and fulfilled many of the functions listed above—but particularly for defining living spaces and for adding texture or interest to a room.

In the mid-1950s, the Aluminum Company of America (Alcoa) initiated a program to promote the use of aluminum in design and architecture, inviting a host of designers to participate, including Isamu Noguchi, Alexander Girard, Charles and Ray Eames, and others. By the early 1960s, Alcoa was marketing its Alshade system, which utilized standard aluminum components assembled into sun screens that were designed to be both functional and ornamental. A promotional brochure[4] was published by Alcoa in 1963—the year of its 75th anniversary—which featured, among other things, the hexagonal- or honeycomb-shaped grille pattern often seen on the *Enterprise*, such as in the engineering section.

Different depths of grille work were available to provide various degrees of screening, and a variety of Alcoa Alumalure baked-enamel color finishes were available. These screens could be affixed to the outside surface of buildings or used internally.

From the 1963 Alcoa sales brochure, showing examples of some of the company's aluminum screen products available during the 1960s. The Alcoa Alshade was a simple system of standard aluminum components assembled into sun screens made of cast aluminum units joined mechanically and used in a variety of ways. One very popular product was the hexagonal pattern (shown in the left middle image), which featured prominently on the *U.S.S. Enterprise*.

Images from *Star Trek* that illustrate the numerous practical and dramatic applications of the decorative grille or room divider are shown below.

Lt. Charlene Masters (Janet MacLachlan), a specialist in dilithium crystallography in engineering in "The Alternative Factor."

"ALUMINUM, THE CHAMELEON MATERIAL, OPENS TO THE DESIGNER AN INEXHAUSTIBLE PALETTE OF FORM, TEXTURE, AND COLOR. IT RESPONDS TO EVERY KNOWN TECHNIQUE OF THE METAL-WORKING ART. YET, THIS EXPRESSIVE MATERIAL FOR BUILDING HAS ONLY JUST BEGUN TO REVEAL ITS POTENTIALS, AND THE ARCHITECT HAS SCARCELY BEGUN TO EXPLOIT THEM."
—ARCHITECT PHILLIP WILL, JR.

The metal hexagonal grillwork in the control room casts evocative shadows on Captain Kirk and Mr. Spock as they attempt to correct Yonada's course in "For the World is Hollow and I Have Touched the Sky."

"You see, it works both ways. I hardly believe you are the injured party." From "The *Enterprise* Incident."

The decorative screen behind Dr. McCoy both separates areas in the guest quarters and provides a textured backdrop for the scenes that play out before it. From "For the World is Hollow and I Have Touched the Sky."

A Morg patiently awaits his ration of "pain and delight." Suspended above is decorative grillwork that may serve a practical function such as ventilation intake or lighting for the underground community. From "Spock's Brain."

A pensive Captain Kirk prior to his trial in "Court Martial." This particular room divider was probably made by the set designers for this episode.

In "Court Martial," the cardiac monitor subtracts the heartbeat signals of everyone present on the bridge to locate Lieutenant Commander Finney, who was presumed dead but actually alive and somewhere on board.

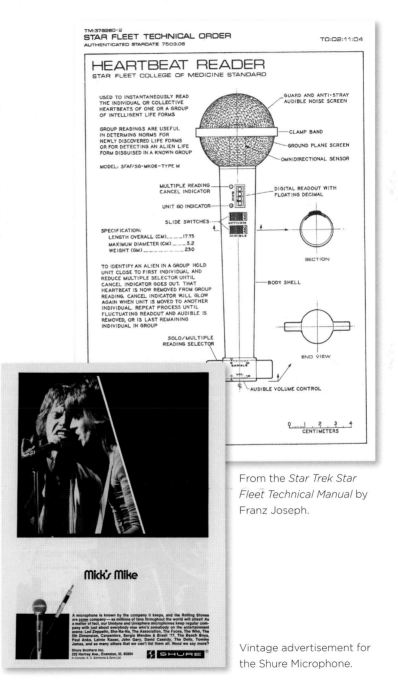

From the *Star Trek Star Fleet Technical Manual* by Franz Joseph.

Upon closer inspection of Dr. McCoy's tray of operating equipment in a previous photo, one sees something that looks like a microphone. It *is* a microphone—at least, it is in the twentieth century. In the *Star Trek Star Fleet Technical Manual*,[3] we learn that this is a cardiac monitor, and that it can detect both individual and collective heartbeats; in cases, it can also be used to differentiate humans from nonhumans.

The microphone was a product of Shure Brothers Inc. in Evanston, Illinois. Available in both the Unidyne and Unisphere models, these microphones, as a vintage advertisement boasted, were used by the likes of the Rolling Stones, the Who, Led Zeppelin, the Carpenters, the Beach Boys, Sha Na Na, and David Cassidy—and, of course, Doctor McCoy.

Vintage advertisement for the Shure Microphone.

AT HOME ON THE *ENTERPRISE*

From occasional views of living quarters on the *U.S.S. Enterprise*, we obtain glimpses into the personal lives and interests of several major characters. Replicating Matt Jefferies' drawing, one set was built on the Desilu Studios soundstage that consisted of a generously sized room divided by a decorative metal screen into two living areas and contained a bed, built-in shelves and cabinets, a built-in vertical wardrobe and dresser that rotated open and shut, minimalistic furniture, and presumably (but not shown) a bathroom. By means of altering the configuration, decor, and lighting techniques, this single versatile set became the cabins of numerous crew members.

Behind Nancy Crater and looming over Dr. McCoy's bed among a selection of other personal items is a ceramic figure, perhaps a talisman rooted in the religious iconography of an early civilization on a distant planet. Rendered in a handmade, almost crude fashion, the figurative sculpture is the work of Hal Fromhold. This same, or a similar, piece may be seen above Captain Kirk's bed in the episode "Obsession."

An Englishman who moved to Vancouver in 1950 to practice ceramics, Hal Fromhold went on to study under ceramicist F. Carlton Ball at USC where he earned a bachelor's degree; he later obtained his MA degree  at Ohio State University. Moving back to Los Angeles, Fromhold set up his own studio and began making his signature work in clay as a potter. Fromhold frequently made figurative sculptures that appear ancient, with such touches as shields, daggers, tablets, and wings. In 1958, he received an award at the Universal Exposition in Brussels.

Matt Jefferies' generic sketch of an officer's quarters.

The salt vampire, now Nancy Crater, preparing to morph into a counterfeit Dr. McCoy. From "The Man Trap."

In "The Tholian Web," we visit Lieutenant Uhura's cabin, perhaps the most distinctively decorated of all the crew-quarters. The primitivism, reflected in the zebra-patterned quilt on her bed and wooden carving on her shelf, is contrasted by a high-end Murano glass bowl from the 1950s and an intricately carved wooden chair in the background, of unknown origin.

Sitting on Uhura's vanity dresser flanking a set of wooden carvings is a pair of matching Italian Empoli decanters. Empoli is discussed in Season Three's "For the World is Hollow and I have Touched the Sky."

The standard set for an officer's quarters takes on a wholly different atmosphere by colored lighting on the walls and decorative screens. Lt. Uhura, holding her uniform, reflects on the missing Captain Kirk, trapped in interphase, in "The Tholian Web."

From "The Tholian Web."

Sears catalog advertisement of Italian glassware.

Yeoman Rand's cabin becomes a scene of violence in "The Enemy Within," when the duplicate of Captain Kirk, created by a malfunctioning transporter and drunk with Saurian brandy, attempts sexual assault—said to be the first such depiction on NBC television and at the time highly controversial.[5,6] We learn in the episode that Rand enjoys abstract painting in her spare time, and collects cultural artifacts from around the galaxy.

If there is a pattern in the officers' tastes, it seems to run toward native art or primitivism. Traveling throughout the galaxy would offer numerous opportunities for collecting souvenirs representing diverse civilizations. In Captain Kirk's quarters, we see a statue of the Aztec god Xōchipilli, who rules over art, dance, games, and flowers. From "Obsession," we know that Kirk also has a ceramic figurine by Hal Fromhold similar to that in Dr. McCoy's quarters.

The Aztec god Xōchipilli.

Note the Saurian brandy decanter Kirk had discarded in front of the room divider. From "The Enemy Within."

From "For the World is Hollow and I have Touched the Sky".

Christine Chapel stands over Spock with compassion and solicitude as he suffers through his *pon farr*. From "Amok Time."

Rarely do we see Spock's personal quarters—the notable exception being in "Amok Time." At first glance, there is little to remark on, with the main living area of his spartan quarters showing only a computer, a 3-D chess set, a tricorder case, and what looks like a molecular-model building set. And, of course, we also see Nurse Chapel's bowl of *plomeek* soup flying through the air and out the door.

Later on in the episode we are given a closer view of Spock's sleeping alcove, and here it gets interesting.: Swords, battle-axes, and knives are displayed—remarkable given that Vulcan culture is known for peace, logic, and learning. Looming over his bed is an incense-burning statue that appears to depict a cross between the Egyptian deity Sekhmet and a Babylonian lamassu. The bronze bust in the corner appears to be ancient Grecian, perhaps a representation of Alexander the Great. Not what one would expect from Spock.

From "Amok Time."

STAR TREK FASHION

Undoubtedly *Star Trek* was heavily influenced by Midcentury Modern design in the set decorations that were used to depict the future. Creative flow can go both ways, however, and the "look" of *Star Trek* itself appeared to inspire trends in 1960s fashion.

This effect can be traced to the minidress that female *Enterprise* crew members wore. In both pilot episodes, "The Cage" and "Where No Man Has Gone Before," women wore black trousers like the men, and loose turtleneck-like tops.[5] Early promotional stills in preparation for the launch of Season One showed these same uniforms. However, by the time the first production episode, "The Corbomite Maneuver," had been filmed, the ensemble had been replaced. This change has been attributed to the influence of Grace Lee Whitney,[6] who played Yeoman Rand—a popular crew member despite having appeared in only eight episodes in Season One. As legend has it, Whitney insisted that costume designer William Ware Theiss replace the stodgy trousers for the female crewmembers with minidresses and black boots—which he did. The result changed the trajectory of 1960s fashion.

Early versions of the *Enterprise* uniforms had male and female crew members in similar attire.

The final fashion look on the starship *Enterprise*.

Note the *Star Trek*-like insignia in the center of the picture. Photo by Yoshi Takata, dated 1967.

Pierre Cardin, the noted French fashion designer, was fascinated by space exploration and the future. In 1964, he launched his Cosmocorps line of clothing celebrating the Space Age that was featured through 1969. The pieces in this collection are notable for their high-energy kinetic feel, nontraditional fabrics such as vinyl and other synthetics, thigh-high boots, and a unisex look featuring zippered sweaters and jumpsuits for men. In 1969, Cardin went so far as to visit NASA in Houston to discuss what clothing styles would be appropriate to wear on the moon.

In 2019, the Brooklyn Museum in New York opened the exhibit *Pierre Cardin: Future Fashion*, curated by Matthew Yokobosky, that included Cardin's Cosmocorps clothing line.[7,8,9] Clear parallels are drawn between some of Cardin's designs (photographed in 1967) and the uniforms worn by female crew members on the *Enterprise*—particularly with the hemlines and the high boots.

Photo by Yoshi Takata, dated 1969.

Are these Cardin fashions *Star Trek*-inspired or the other way around? You be the judge.

As we assess through our present-day lens the past predictions of the future, the lines between what is retro and what is futuristic become exceedingly blurred.

REGINALD POLLACK

Behind Kirk is a painting attributed to the midcentury painter Reginald Pollack.

Captain Kirk, Dr. McCoy, and Mr. Spock are on a small planet in the Omega system searching for ryetalyn, a raw material necessary for the antidote for Rigellian fever which has broken out on the *Enterprise*. There, they encounter a mysterious individual named Flint who, as it turns out, is immortal: having been, at various times on Earth, Methuselah, Solomon, Alexander the Great, and Lazarus—as well as Leonardo da Vinci, William Shakespeare, Johannes Brahms, and others. Consequently, his castle is filled with original but unknown works of art, music, and literature never before seen on Earth.

More recently, he must have also been the mid-twentieth-century artist Reginald Pollack, as Spock identifies examples of Pollack's work on Flint's wall.

At a very young age, Reginald Pollack was taken to MoMA by his father. It was there he taught himself how to sketch. After serving in World War II and then making window displays in

New York, Pollack moved to Paris to study art. While there, he attended the Académie de la Grande Chaumière. He was influenced by the artists Alberto Giacametti, Fernand Léger, and Man Ray. Famous sculptor Constantin Brâncuşi was one of his mentors. During his twelve years in Paris, Pollack was one of the founding members of the Galerie Huit, the first gallery in Paris run by Americans. In the 1960s, Pollack moved back to New York and then eventually Los Angeles. He continued producing art until his death in 1998. His work is in the permanent collections at MoMA, the Whitney Museum of American Art, and the Smithsonian American Art Museum.

1963 work by Pollack entitled *Perhaps the Only Goal on Earth Toward Which Mankind is Striving*.

BIOGRAPHIES
PROPERTY MASTER

IRVING FEINBERG, property master for *Star Trek*, was born in Illinois in 1909. His involvement spanned virtually the entire series. An employee of Desilu Studios, he also served as property master for 30 episodes of *The Untouchables* (1959–61).

Feinberg was known for being quick, innovative, and resourceful. His responsibilities included all props used in the episodes, including phasers, tricorders, communicators, operating utensils, and salt shakers. So ubiquitous was Feinberg's work that Dr. McCoy's medical scanner was termed a Feinberger on the set.

Feinberg died in Los Angeles in 1991.

1 Joseph, Franz. *Star Trek Star Fleet Technical Manual* page TO:02:11:14. New York: Ballantine, 1975.

2 Marshall, Ron; Marshall, Barbara. "Concrete Screen Block: The Power of Pattern." Palm Springs Preservation Foundation, 2018.

3 Joseph, Franz. op cit page TO:02:11:04

4 Bass, Saul. "Aluminum: The Architect's Metal." Aluminum Company of America marketing brochure, Pittsburgh PA, 1963.

5 Gurian, Gerald. *To Boldly Go: Rare Photos from the TOS Soundstage—Season One*. Las Vegas: Minkatek, 2016.

6 Cushman, Mark; Osborn, Susan. *These Are the Voyages: TOS Season One*. San Diego: Jacobs Brown, 2013.

7 Farago, Jason. "A Designer's Space-Age Daydreams." the *New York Times*, 23 August 2019, Section C, p. 12.

8 Farago, Jason. "Pierre Cardin's Space-Age Fashion Takes Us Back to the Future." https://www.nytimes.com/2019/08/22/arts/design/pierre-cardin-brooklyn-museum-review.html.

9 "Pierre Cardin Exhibition Aims to Revive the Designer's Once-Bold Image." *The Star*, 25 July 2019. https://www.thestar.com.my/lifestyle/style/2019/07/25/pierre-cardin-future-fashion-brooklyn-museum/

SEASON THREE

LEFT Elda chairs by Joe Colombo.

THE *ENTERPRISE* INCIDENT

Season 3 • **Production Sequence** 59 • **Air Date** September 27, 1968 • **Stardate** 5027.3
Art Director Walter M. "Matt" Jefferies • **Set Decorator** John M. Dwyer • **Property Master** Irving A. Feinberg

SYNOPSIS

Espionage is the word when Captain Kirk ostensibly goes rogue and directs the *Enterprise* into Romulan space, violating the Federation's peace treaty with the Romulan Empire. Unbeknownst to the crew, however, Kirk and Spock have been tasked by Starfleet to obtain the Romulans' cloaking device, which renders their ships invisible to both sensors and sight, giving them an enormous advantage in military engagements and espionage actions. The cover story of "instrument failure and navigational error" on the *Enterprise* allows Kirk and Spock to board the Romulan flagship, where Spock provides a distraction while Kirk searches for the cloaking device.

Noted actress Joanne Linville chews up the scenery in her portrayal of the tightly wound Romulan commander—particularly in the steamy sequences with the admiring Spock. This interesting relationship poses the question "Did he or didn't he [lie]?" of which Vulcans are renowned for being incapable. Based on their parting exchange in the turbolift, we must conclude that there is definitely something going on: As they are about to part ways, Spock says, "You underestimate yourself, Commander [...] military secrets are the most fleeting of all. I hope you and I exchanged something more permanent," to which she replies, "It will be our secret."

▶ ELDA CHAIR FOR COMFORT · ITALY · 1963
DESIGNER: JOE COLOMBO

The Romulans' apparent affinity for elegant design belies their otherwise warlike ferocity. The commander's personal quarters feature several fine examples of midcentury art. In one scene, she envelops herself in an oversized, space-age chair from which she shoots her verbal barbs. The black leather foam padding of the Elda chair surrounds her like a dark and sinister cloak.

"The matter of trespass into Romulan space is one of galactic import—a violation of treaties."

Joe Colombo's Elda chair.

Industrial designer Joe Colombo attended the Accademia di Belle Arti di Brera in Milan and then was an architecture student at the Politecnico di Milano. Active as a painter and sculptor in the 1950s, Colombo joined several art groups. Thereafter, he gave up painting to pursue his design career and run his family business. It is there that he learned to experiment with materials and construction. In 1962, Colombo opened his own design firm. The Elda chair, named after his wife, was one of his first designs.

A furniture system was developed, called the Additional Living System, that included lamps, alarm clocks, wristwatches, and dinnerware; more furniture soon followed. Besides the Elda chair, there's the Tubo lounge chair, the Universale chair, the Brillio stool series and the Boby trolley cart. An Elda chair is in the permanent collection at MoMA.

"NOW, IF THE ELEMENTS NECESSARY TO HUMAN EXISTENCE COULD BE PLANNED WITH THE SOLE REQUIREMENTS OF MANEUVERABILITY AND FLEXIBILITY . . . THEN WE WOULD CREATE AN INHABITABLE SYSTEM THAT COULD BE ADAPTED TO ANY SITUATION IN SPACE AND TIME."

—JOE COLOMBO

▶ BRUTALIST RING · USA · 1960s
DESIGNER: ATTRIBUTED TO ARTHUR PEPPER

The Romulan commander wears dangling opalescent earrings as well as a Brutalist ring, made of bronze fragments reminiscent of a ring attributed to jewelers Arthur Pepper or Hungarian designer Pal Kepenyes in the 1960s.

"Commander, your attire is not only more appropriate, it should actually stimulate our conversation."

"If you will give me a moment, the soldier will transform herself into a woman."

▶ 'RAINDROPS' WALL MIRROR FOR ARTISAN HOUSE · USA · 1968
DESIGNER: CURTIS JERÉ

The Romulan commander, taken by the fact that Spock is Vulcan, invites him to her quarters where they become entwined in a game of mutual manipulation. Above them is a round Brutalist mirror featuring metal "raindrops" that encompass it.

Curtis Jeré, or C. Jeré, is the nom de plume of Jerry Fels and his brother-in-law, Kurt Freiler, who founded Artisan House in Los Angeles in 1963, through which all Jeré pieces were sold. Fels, formerly of the Art Students League in New York, was head of design, with Freiler as head of production. Working with materials such as brass, copper, and bronze, Curtis Jeré was known for creating sculptures of animals, street scenes, foliage, lamps, and oversized kitchen utensils, mostly in the Brutalist aesthetic.

FOR THE WORLD IS HOLLOW AND I HAVE TOUCHED THE SKY

Season 3 • **Production Sequence** 65 • **Air Date** November 8, 1968 • **Stardate** 5476.3
Art Director Walter M. "Matt" Jefferies • **Set Decorator** John M. Dwyer • **Property Master** Irving A. Feinberg

SYNOPSIS

The *Enterprise* encounters a sort of inside-out world called Yonada—actually a spaceship disguised as an asteroid. The inhabitants, who live on the inner surface, are unaware that their ancestors, fleeing a dying solar system, had built the vessel, launched it 10,000 years ago, and put it on autopilot toward a new home. However, the guidance system went awry and they are now on a collision course with the populated planet Daran V. Further complicating the plot is Dr. McCoy, who, diagnosed with a fatal hematologic disease, falls in love with the high priestess Natira (played by Kate Woodville) and decides to live out his remaining time with her. Veteran actor Jon Lormer, in a bad wig, plays an old man who

had discovered the secret of Yonada and, after reciting the name of the episode, falls dead—victim to a subcutaneous microchip that punishes blasphemers. Lormer also played one of the imaginary crash survivors in "The Cage" and was one of the townspeople in "The Return of the Archons."

This is not the only *Star Trek* episode in which the descendants of an ancient civilization have lost the skills necessary to control and repair the technology left behind by their ancestors—a cautionary tale for all of us. Natira poses a question to the Oracle that is eerily relevant to us in today's world of disinformation: "Is truth not truth for all?"

Either by accident or as a gag by the set decorator, the glass stopper is inserted upside down.

▶ EMPOLI GLASS · ITALY · 1960s

After the *Enterprise* crew members are deemed acceptable as visitors by the Oracle, Natira permits Captain Kirk and Mr. Spock to take a walking tour of the underground community. Natira stays behind to become better acquainted with Dr. McCoy. The guest quarters reflect the tasteful decor found on Yonada, which includes a fine example of Empoli glassware.

Empoli is a region southwest of Florence in Tuscany, Italy. Making its namesake green glass—Empoli Verde, named for the color that occurs in the sands of the region—Empoli has been producing glass since the fourteenth century. Empoli glassware such as decanters, vases, tumblers, bottles, and plates, is often confused with both Murano glass from Venice and products from the American glass company Blenko. Empoli is known for its thin-walled glass, as opposed to Blenko's thicker-walled products. In the 1950s and '60s, Empoli began producing an array of brightly colored glass, mainly for the American market.

Empoli vases with the stoppers right-side up, from Zus Korsten, Haarlem, Netherlands.

▶ RYA · SWEDEN/FINLAND/NORWAY/DENMARK · 1960s

After Dr. McCoy marries Natira, the Instrument of Obedience is implanted into his temple. When he tries to contact the *Enterprise* with his discoveries, he sets off the device and collapses in agony, conveniently falling onto a plush *rya*, or rug—exactly where the old man had previously collapsed and died. The vertiginous swirls of blue, deep purple, and green evoke an exploding asteroid.

One of the oldest types of Scandinavian rugs, the rya (or *ryijy*, meaning rug) dates back to the ninth and tenth centuries. They were first presented to Norse people by merchants. This high-piled wool rug was originally used by seal hunters and fisherman and later as bedding in Sweden, often as part of a bride's dowry—and was later displayed like a tapestry. In eighteenth-century Finland, ryas became more decorative. It wasn't until the 1960s and '70s that they became popular in the United States and were used as actual area rugs. Similar to a shag rug in thickness, the ryas were offered in myriad color ways, sizes, designs, and patterns that appeared more like paintings.

Oblivious to their fate, the colonists of Yonada can take comfort in the high-end art and furnishings that surround them. The guest quarters for the *Enterprise* officers reflect this opulence: besides the ryas and the Empoli glass, one sees Brutalist wall hangings, platform beds and tables made of green marble, and various other antiquities. Some of these objects are of unidentified designers; others were perhaps constructed by the set designers. The sinuous lines of these treasures contrast sharply with the geometric hieroglyphic symbols on the panels inside the Oracle Room, which the people on Yonada are unable to read anymore.

BIOGRAPHIES
SET DECORATOR

JOSEPH STONE, a set decorator on *Star Trek*, had a career that spanned three decades. He worked on twelve episodes of *Star Trek*—all during Season Two, including "Metamorphosis," an episode with a plethora of midcentury pieces. Besides this, his television credits also include series such as *Honey West*, *The Man from U.N.C.L.E.*, *It Takes a Thief*, *Alias Smith and Jones*, *McCloud*, *Ironside*, *Quincy, M.E.*, *Centennial*, *B.J. and the Bear*, *Fame*, and *Hardcastle and McCormick*. In addition to his work on *Star Trek*, Stone won a Primetime Emmy for his work on the series *Fame* (1982) and was nominated four additional times.

"THE TRUTH OF YONADA IS YOUR TRUTH. THERE CAN BE NO OTHER FOR YOU. REPENT YOUR DISOBEDIENCE."

—THE ORACLE

THE CLOUD MINDERS

Season 3 • **Production Sequence** 74 • **Air Date** February 28, 1969 • **Stardate** 5818.4
Art Director Walter M. Jefferies • **Set Decorator** John M. Dwyer • **Property Master** Irving A. Feinberg

SYNOPSIS

This episode portrays the timeless allegory of class warfare, bigotry, and prejudice. On the planet Ardana, the Troglytes are forced to live and work as miners on the inhospitable surface of the planet, where a toxic gas slows their mental functions and renders them violent. The people of Stratos, meanwhile, live in an ethereal city far from the noxious planet surface, suspended among the clouds by means of antigravity; this city is dedicated to art and intellectual pursuits.

In violation of the Prime Directive of cultural noninterference, Captain Kirk and Mr. Spock trigger a social crisis as they seek to both instill equality and justice, and secure an antidote to a botanical plague ravaging a Federation planet elsewhere.

Kirk and Spock find the planet Ardana to be a world of contradictions: The leisure and affluence in the city of Stratos contrast sharply with the squalid conditions of the miners on Ardana's surface. The refined demeanor of the Stratos dwellers also belies the ease with which they torture those whom they consider Disruptors.

Also, in contrast to the evolved and refined culture of Stratos is the Brutalist art that predominates, which features raw, jagged, and angular abstractions of welded, metal fixtures that adorn the halls of the city. Brutalism as a recognized aesthetic in architecture and art is discussed in more detail in the "Brutalism" and "Futuristic Architecture" chapters.

"This troubled planet is a place of the most violent contrasts. Those who receive the rewards are totally separated from those who shoulder the burdens."

▶ RIBBON CHAIR FOR ARTIFORT · FRANCE/THE NETHERLANDS · 1965.
DESIGNER: PIERRE PAULIN

Pierre Paulin was a French furniture and interior designer who first trained as a ceramicist in Vallauris. He attended the prestigious École Camondo in Paris. His furniture designs gained acclaim with the design of the Mushroom chair (1960).

The Ribbon chair is considered one of Paulin's most iconic designs for Dutch furniture company Artifort, in Maastricht. His other chair designs include the Orange Slice chair and the Tongue chair, all of which, like the Ribbon chair, incorporate the use of metal frames with rubber webbing padded with foam.

A pair of Pierre Paulin's Ribbon chairs.

Vintage advertisement for Paulin's Ribbon chair, marketed by Artifort.

"DESIGN IS A COLLECTIVE PRACTICE
AT THE SERVICE OF THE PUBLIC."
—PIERRE PAULIN

Behind Mr. Spock and Captain Kirk is an example of the abundance of art that graces Stratos—a metal spray sculpture.

Tom McCallister spray sculpture.

▶ SPRAY SCULPTURE · USA · 1966
ATTRIBUTION: TOM MCALLISTER, DAVE GOODMAN, OR HARRY BERTOIA

Little is known about either Tom McAllister or Dave Goodman, except that McAllister was based in Tarzana, California, and created his kinetic metal spray sculpture in 1966.

The origin of this sculpture begins with the designer and sculptor Harry Bertoia. A student at Michigan's famous Cranbrook Academy of Art, Bertoia began his career making steel sculptures, jewelry, and monotypes. He later made designs for Florence and Hans Knoll for their company Knoll, Inc. During this time, Bertoia produced his most iconic design, the Diamond chair. Besides making the kinetic spray sculpture, he is credited with myriad commissions he did for public institutions nationwide.

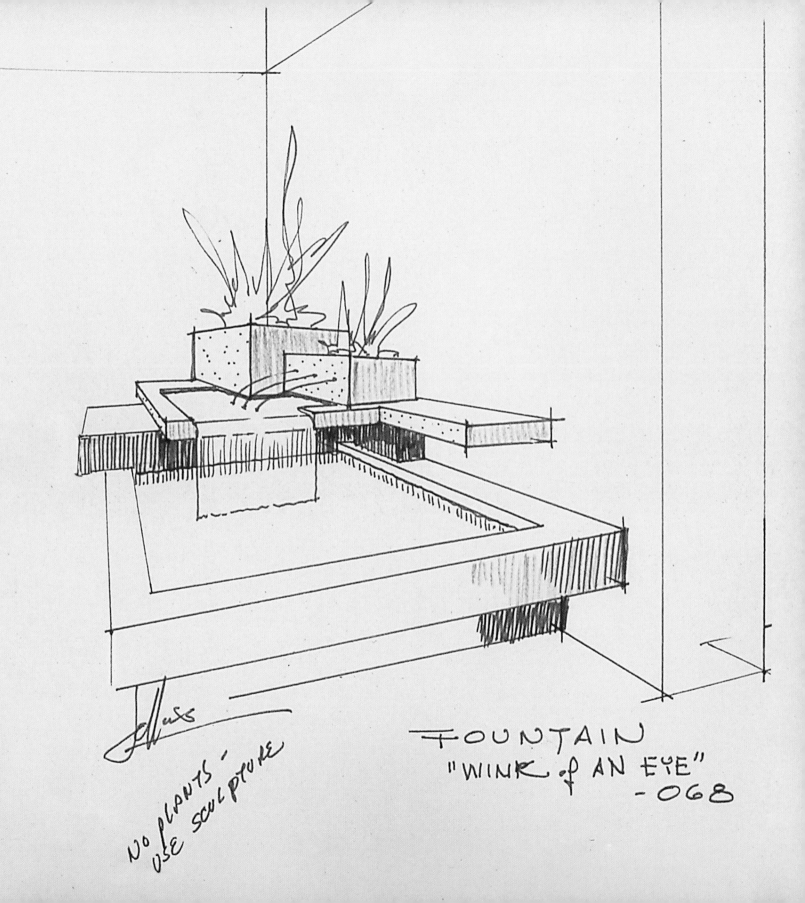

NO PLANTS -
USE SCULPTURE

FOUNTAIN
"WINK of AN EYE"
-068

BRUTALISM

Béton Brut. Raw concrete. Architect Le Corbusier coined the term in relation to the construction of his Unité d' Habitation building in 1952, thus spawning an architectural movement popularized from the 1950s to the 1970s. A thoroughly modern movement characterized by exposed materials such as raw concrete, Brutalism is rooted in Europe. There are numerous examples of Brutalist architecture throughout the world, particularly in England, where the movement flourished in large part due to the postwar housing shortage.

The Royal National Theater in London is another example of Brutalist architecture. Designed in 1976 by architect Denys Lasdun, the building exemplifies the principles of *Béton Brut* for its mass of exposed concrete. Other examples include Le Corbusier's radical and elegant design for the Notre-Dame du Hait Chapel in Ronchamp, France in 1955, or the more extreme Brutalist fortress-like cathedral known as the Wotruba Church in Vienna, Austria, created by architect Fritz Wotruba and built between 1974 and 1976.

Le Corbusier. Unite d' Habitation. 1952

Le Corbusier. Notre-Dame du Hait Chapel. 1955.

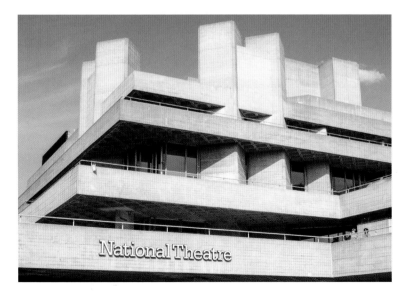

Denys Lasdun. The Royal National Theater. 1976.

Fritz Wotruba. Wotruba Church. 1974–76.

Alison & Peter Smithson. Robin Hood Gardens. 1969-72.

Paul Rudolph. Yale School of Architecture (now Rudolph Hall).

From the Robin Hood Gardens (1969-1972) in East London by British New Brutalist founders Alison and Peter Smithson, to the Yale School of Architecture in New Haven, Connecticut, by American architect Paul Rudolph, each example illustrates an honesty of structure: unadorned, uncomplicated, and uncompromising. Brutalism came out of Modernism as a new language in art and architecture. All of the structures illustrated herein share the same monochromatic palette—a recurring theme of both Brutalist architecture and art.

Less is known, however, about the origins of Brutalism in the decorative arts. Several designers of note, discussed below, exemplify the Brutalist movement, and whose works distinctly resemble various sculptures seen in several episodes of *Star Trek*. These designers—Silas Seandel, Paul Evans, William Bowie, and Klaus Ihlenfeld—illustrate the principles of Brutalism: the use of raw exposed materials, generally metal.

Silas Seandel.
Wall Sculpture.

▶ PAUL EVANS · FURNITURE DESIGNER AND SCULPTOR

Paul Evans studied at the prestigious Cranbrook Academy of Art in Bloomfield, Michigan. Beginning in the 1950s, Evans worked in steel and copper, making finely crafted hand-made furniture. He eventually designed for the company Directional Furniture, where he produced several furniture lines of the same level of quality. Such designs included cabinets, tables, coffee tables, credenzas, and chairs, as well as custom pieces. Rooted in the Brutalist aesthetic, Paul Evans' work is highly collectible.

▶ SILAS SEANDEL · SCULPTOR

Silas Seandel studied economics and sculpture at the University of Pennsylvania. He opened his studio in 1963, making sculptures for architects, interior designers, and engineers. Over the course of his illustrious career, he completed countless commissions for a multitude of corporations, including AT&T, Ford Motor Company, Johnson & Johnson, Standard Oil, and Pfizer Corporation.

Paul Evans sculpture.

Anonymous
Brutalist
sculpture.

Paul Evans Brutalist table base.

▶ WILLIAM BOWIE · SCULPTOR

Among his contemporaries Harry Bertoia, Silas Seandel, and Curtis Jeré, Bowie is considered one of the leading designers of sculpted metal. Making mosaics and stained glass in New York City in the 1950s, he opened his first studio there in 1958, Bowie eventually switched to working in metal. He is the recipient of numerous awards and commissions.

Harry Bertoia. Sonambient sculpture.

William Bowie sculpture.

▶ KLAUS IHLENFELD · SCULPTOR

Klaus Ihlenfeld studied in his native city of Berlin in the 1950s at the Academy of Fine Arts. His teacher was sculptor Hans Uhlmann. It was in 1957 when he traveled to the United States and began working as a studio assistant to sculptor and designer Harry Bertoia (see "The Cloud Minders" episode.)

Klaus Ihlenfeld. "Lily pads" coffee table.

The works of Curtis Jeré, mentioned above, appear both in Season One's "The Conscience of the King" and in Season Three's "The *Enterprise* Incident." In the authors' examination of *Star Trek* episodes for identifying notable objects, more and more examples of Brutalism emerged, compelling us to dedicate a separate chapter to this topic.

Numerous examples of Brutalist art live within the walls of futurist cities on distant planets, in a host of episodes throughout the *Star Trek* universe. As stated in the introduction from an interview with set decorator John M. Dwyer, he either found various pieces of art in stores, or in some cases the prop department made the art themselves. It is speculative as to what was the driving motivation for placing such a large amount of Brutalist decorative art in *Star Trek*. Upon closer examination, a pattern emerges: the Brutalist aesthetic is in marked contrast to the other furnishings utilized. Furthermore, the placement of Brutalist objects is quite often associated with cultures engaged in conflict, from the hatred of internal class warfare to the angst of interplanetary strife.

In "The Conscience of the King," a Brutalist sculpture is seen atop a table in Dr. Leighton's home, portraying an aquatic scene of fish swimming amongst strands of seaweed. The sculpture's raw, jagged material contrasts sharply with the rest of Leighton's midcentury furnishings. (See "The Conscience of the King" episode.)

Most conspicuous at the beam-down reception area on Starbase 11 in "The Menagerie" is a large, unyielding Brutalist sculpture greeting Kirk, Spock, and McCoy. The anonymously designed sculpture consists of a collection of circular gestures intertwined between sharp, jagged pieces of denuded metal. It is one of our first glimpses of the Starbase. Once again, the sculpture is in strong aesthetic contrast to the modernist surroundings. (see the "Futurist Architecture" chapter.)

From "The Menagerie."

From "The Conscience of the King."

The studio set for the Starbase 11 beam-down point was reworked to become the same element for the planet Eminiar VII in "A Taste of Armageddon." But a wholly different Brutalist sculpture awaits the *Enterprise* crew: Due to its singular position in the city with little else around it, this assemblage of twisted, torch-cut metal in rising, flame-like shapes, is perhaps symbolic of the planet's current political turmoil.

From "A Taste of Armageddon."

With the Enterprise delegation about to materialize, this Brutalist sculpture is seen in a long shot with the Eminiar VII cityscape beyond. With its intricate detailing and large mass, the sculpture resembles the work of the Brutalist sculptors Curtis Jeré and Silas Seandel. However, the actual attribution of the Eminiar VII piece is unknown.

"A Taste of Armageddon" features several other examples of Brutalism, many within the quarters of Anan 7. In the immediate foreground of a scene between Anan 7 and Captain Kirk is a black Brutalist table-top sculpture, again made of raw metal—unadorned and untamed. On the wall behind the characters is a large sculpture of the same materials. These two pieces are in contrast to the elegant, midcentury modern pieces that occupy the space. Does Anan 7 have these strategically placed so as to intimidate Captain Kirk? As in most Brutalist sculptures, the pieces are monochromatic, contrasting with both Anan 7's gilded toga and deep red pant leg, and his suave but brutish behavior.

In another scene, Kirk is standing beside a gold figurative sculpture and a Tom Greene hanging lamp. (See the "A Taste of Armageddon" episode.) The Brutalist figure, naked and raw, seems to confront Kirk and to foreshadow the impending conflict.

From "A Taste of Armageddon."

Bronze figurative sculpture. 1960s.

Tom Greene hanging lamp.

From "Operation -- Annihilate!"

Within the city of Deneva in "Operation -- Annihilate!" lie several Brutalist accoutrements. Sam Kirk's laboratory is populated by a host of midcentury modern furnishings. The tall conspicuous piece on the right side of the room echoes the work of Silas Seandel, with its grouping of intersecting sheets of metal rising to a plateau. Two additional smaller sculptures atop the midcentury modern desk on the left are but mere figurative abstractions, possibly placed to fill the scene by adding depth and dimension. Were these sculptures placed by the prop masters to reflect the violent emotional states of the citizens caused by insidious single-celled parasites?

From a crashed ship using salvaged parts, Zefram Cochrane's architecturally notable home emerged in "Metamorphosis." (See the "Futurist Architecture" chapter.) Not only has Cochrane managed to build beautifully designed furnishings for his dwelling, he has also lent his artistic hand to numerous Brutalist sculptures adorning the interior walls.

Two such salient wall sculptures are hanging in the main room of his shelter. The larger of the two is attributed to the designer Silas Seandel: a composition consisting of strips of coarse torch-cut metal with seemingly-random holes burned through the material. The Brutalist sculpture is evocative not only of Seandel's 1960s work, but also that of designer Tom Greene. (See "A Taste of Armageddon" in "Season One"). Similarly, Greene also torch-cut many of his pieces and created the patina of a worn, salvaged look for his famous lighting fixtures of the same period.

The other Brutalist wall sculpture also mirrors salvaged parts from Cochrane's ship: a monochromatic collection of metal pieces bonded together to form the whole configuration. Much like Anan 7's quarters in "A Taste of Armageddon," both Brutalist pieces are in stark contrast to the inhabitants' surrounding furniture. Considering the narrative of "Metamorphosis," it seems logical that Cochrane would create abstract, amorphous pieces reminiscent of the Companion.

Silas Seandel. Wall Sculpture.

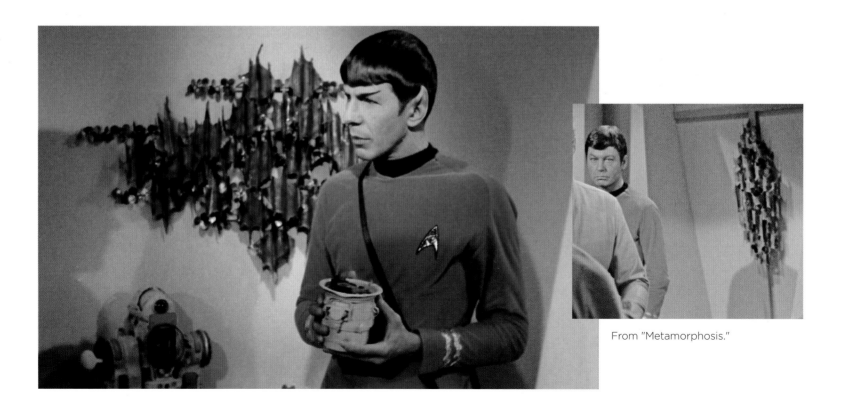

From "Metamorphosis."

A Brutalist figurative sculpture is seen on the planet Scalos at the beginning of the episode "Wink of an Eye," kneeling as if deep in thought and contemplation atop a water fountain. Captain Kirk and Mr. Spock arrive on the planet to discover the planet's inhabitants absent. The sculpture is initially the only representation of humanity.

Also of note is Matt Jefferies' sketch of a water fountain from "Wink of an Eye," which exemplifies the minimalism of Brutalist architecture. (See this chapter's title page.)

From "The Empath."

From "Wink of an Eye."

Deep within the chambers of Minara II in "The Empath," Captain Kirk, Mr. Spock, and Dr. McCoy find unmanned computers and machinery. As they walk through this deserted space, they encounter a cluster of translucent rods beside a tree-shaped Brutalist sculpture. Although dimly lit, the piece has the characteristics of untreated metal and appears jagged and untamed. As yet another study in contrasts, the anonymous sculpture is the converse of the highly modern and technologically advanced computers systems seen in the room. No attribution is available for this Brutalist piece.

In "Requiem for Methuselah," Flint's home has an impressive collection of art and sculpture. On one wall is a Brutalist sculpture made of assembled pieces of cut brass. It hangs among a veritable gallery of masterpieces, including a painting ostensibly by Leonardo da Vinci, as well as a Reginald Pollack painting. (See the "Set Decoration, Props, and Fashion" chapter.) Is the sculpture a harbinger to the unfolding conflict between Flint and Captain Kirk?

From "Requiem for Methuselah."

We end with the city of Stratos in Season Three's "The Cloud Minders," which was also discussed in the corresponding chapter, and in the Futurist Architecture chapter. The cloud city of Stratos is home to some of the most notable examples of Brutalist decorative arts of any episode. Sculptures both large and small were installed within the many spaces throughout the episode, including the Counsel Gallery adjacent to the beam-down point. Much like on the planet Eminiar VII, the *Enterprise* crew are greeted by two very grand Brutalist sculptures: One is cut in the shape of a single flame, while the other is an elaborate and elegant arrangement of what appear to be wings of a butterfly. After Captain Kirk and Mr. Spock's introduction to Plasus' daughter, Droxine, they pass carefully curated sculptures of the gallery—every piece a contemplation and study of Brutalism as art.

The guest sleeping chamber is dressed with several sculptures, including a bird-like, wispy table piece next to the bed. Beside the Pierre Paulin-designed Ribbon chair (see "The Cloud Minders" episode), is a Christ-like figurative piece. In another scene is a massive wall sculpture, appearing like a glittering network of stars—oversized and enveloping the room.

From "The Cloud Minders."

Through the generosity of private *Star Trek* collector Gerald Gurian, the authors were given access to the original sketches of art director Walter M. "Matt" Jefferies. Perusing his concept sketches and storyboards, the origin of the Brutalist influence in *Star Trek* became clear. Particularly in Season Three's "The Cloud Minders," for which Jefferies made numerous sketches, Brutalism was clearly influencing both the architecture of Stratos and the artwork that he specified. As seen in his drawings, Jeffries deliberately drew specific art pieces to populate the various sets. The architecture itself echoes Brutalism in its depiction and renderings of geometric solid shapes. Examples of the Jefferies sketches illustrating his influence on the episode are given below.

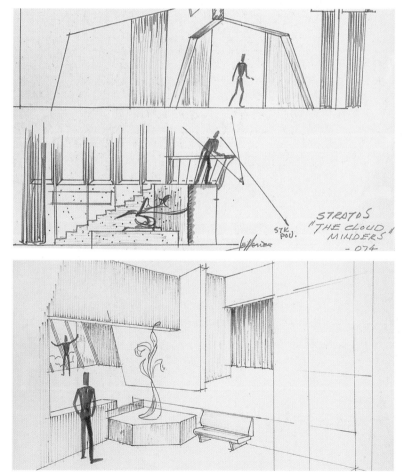

Matt Jefferies' sketches for the guest quarters on Stratos. From "The Cloud Minders."

Matt Jefferies' concept sketches for the balcony and reception chamber on Stratos. From "The Cloud Minders."

The prominent inclusion of Brutalist art in the cloud city of Stratos raises several questions. Why would a culture so dedicated to harmony, symmetry, and intellectualism be drawn to the harsh and jagged asymmetry of Brutalism? Does the art echo the cloud dwellers' intolerant attitudes toward the Troglytes? Was the use of this raw and unadorned art serendipitous, or was it deliberate? These questions remain unanswered, as no existing production notes are available to explain the intentions of either the episode's author of those of the art department.

MIDCENTURY ADVERTISING

Postwar Los Angeles was fertile ground for experimentation in all facets of commerce, including but not limited to architecture, design, art, and the aerospace industry. The city was looked upon as a place of inspiration and ideas by the rest of the country and eventually the world. As Los Angeles grew in population, so too did contemporary furniture stores catering to the more sophisticated tastes of buyers. Stores like Pier 1 Imports, Da Imports, and Michael's Contemporary Furniture specialized in showcasing innovative and modern furnishings from all over the world by a myriad of renowned designers.

The following advertisements all originally appeared in the *Los Angeles Time Home* magazine. They offer a window into 1960s Los Angeles furniture stores from which the decorators John M. Dwyer, Carl F. Biddiscombe, Marvin March, and Joseph Stone would rent furnishings and art to appear on *Star Trek*. In two such ads for the stores Mel Brown and Aaron Schultz, the furniture piece "Mr. Chair," featured in the Season Two episode "Assignment: Earth," appears.

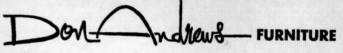

Discover all the newest ways to create more room space . . .

custom • wall

free standing
units shown 72" wide,
3 poles, 8 shelves
choice of 4 finishes

$107⁵⁰

THE WEST'S LEADING CONTEMPORARY HOME FURNISH

michaels
contemporary furniture

LOS ANGELES
601 N. Western
HO 2-2283

WESTWWOOD VILLAGE
1035 Glendon Ave.
GR. 7-7747

VAN NUYS
14640 Victory Blvd.
West of Van Nuys Blvd.
ST. 0-9875

HAWTH
12627
North
SP. 2-

Mon. & Fri. 9:30 to 9:30; Tues., Wed., Thurs., Sat

today, sunday 12 to 5 • interior decors

fall decorating
the contemporary way

Sculptured teak or walnut imported rocker with a selection of
fine materials to enhance any
room.

Mon. & Fri.
9:30 to 9:30,
Tues., Wed.,
Thurs., Sat. 9:30 to 6

Today Sunday 12 to 5

michaels
contemporary furniture

LOS ANGELES
601 N. Western Ave.
HO 2-2283

WESTWOOD VILLAGE
1035 Glendon Ave.
GR. 7-7747

PASADENA
820 E. Colorado Blvd.
MU. 1-0359

VAN NUYS
14640 Victory Blvd.
west of Van Nuys Blvd.
ST. 0-9875

INTERIOR DECORATING AND TERMS AVAILABLE • THE WEST'S LEADING CONTEMPORARY HOME FURNISHER

148

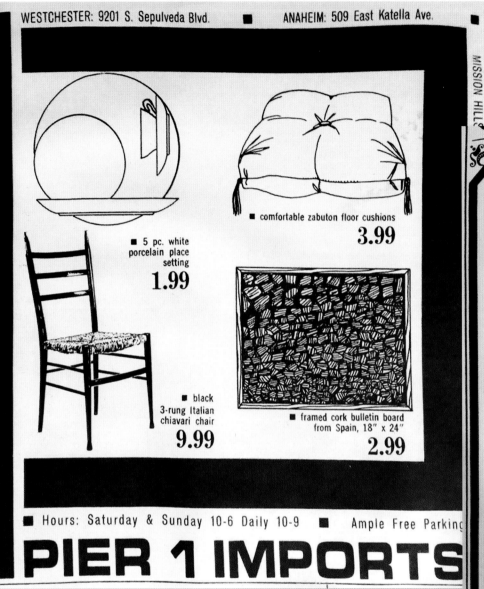

150

GENUINE WALNUT FREE-STANDING WALL UNITS

The wonderful world of wall units opens a new dimension in decorating. Add personality, distinction and versatility to your home with any variety of multiple combinations—free-standing, with movable components, so you can change your decor as you like. Each unit is a spacious 32"— bring your room measurements for a custom-planned creation from a single-starter piece to a magnificent full grouping with chest, desk, cabinets, shelves and display units.

Complete **$498.**

EACH UNIT AVAILABLE SEPARATELY

Complete **$99.**   Complete **$259.**

international home furnishings

OPEN TODAY, SUNDAY 11-5

THE CHAIRS OF TOMORROW

AT INTERNATIONAL

TODAY

LOS ANGELES 466-4415
641 N. Western (Just So. of Melrose)

PASADENA 449-6511
25-27 S. El Molino (Adj. Pas. Playhs.)
DAILY, SAT. 10-6/FRI. 10-9/SUN. 11-5
L.A. CLOSED WED./PAS., RIV. TU., WED.

RIVERSIDE 683-4022
CLEARANCE CENTER
4049 Main St. (Opp. City Court House)
IT'S WORTH THE TRIP

CATALOG OF OBJECTS

Following is an indexed summary of items featured in this book, organized alphabetically by designer. This index is by no means exhaustive: there were many worthwhile items whose respective designer we were unable to identify, although some of these are included if the manufacturer was known. Interesting items that were built by the set designers of *Star Trek* are not included, nor are one-of-a-kind works of art or sculpture. The list focuses on items produced for retail to the public.

Due to the expedience of rapid acquisition, the *Star Trek* set decorators sourced most of the items from US-based manufacturers. However, there are notable exceptions: the Nordic countries (particularly Denmark and Sweden), Italy, and Germany are well represented. Also interesting is the fact that most of these items were introduced in the 1960s—some in the very year that the particular episode featuring the item was filmed. Hence, the public might have seen these items for the very first time on *Star Trek*.

Season One appears to be most heavily laden with high-end midcentury modern pieces, thanks to the work of the set decorators Marvin March and Carl Biddiscombe. This is followed by Season Two, due in large to the single episodes "Assignment: Earth" (set decorator: John Dwyer) and "Metamorphosis" (set decorator: Joseph Stone).

Want to make your home look futuristic like the *U.S.S. Enterprise*? Some of these items are still issued by the original manufacturer. Still others are available as reissues or replicas. Most may be found on the secondary market from internet sites, antique stores, estate sales, and the like. Happy shopping!

DESIGNER	MANUFACTURER	COUNTRY OF ORIGIN	ITEM	ERA	EPISODE(S)	PAGE	
BAUGHMAN, MILO	Thayer Coggin	USA	Swivel Rocker Club Chair	1960s	The Conscience of the King	41	
BORSANI, OSVALDO	Techno	Italy	Boomerang Executive T-series Desk	1954	Assignment: Earth	90	
BURKE, MAURICE	Burke Inc.	USA	Pedestal or "Tulip" Furniture	1960s	All episodes	17	
COLOMBO, JOE	Comfort	Italy	Elda Chair	1963	The *Enterprise* Incident	119	
CRESSEY, DAVID	Architectural Pottery	USA	Stoneware Ceramic Vessel	ca. 1964	A Taste of Armageddon	50	

DESIGNER	MANUFACTURER	COUNTRY OF ORIGIN	ITEM	ERA	EPISODE(S)	PAGE	
CURRY, BILL	Design Line Inc.	USA	Columnlite Models S, G, and C-4	ca. 1965	The Conscience of the King	39	
CURRY, BILL	Design Line Inc.	USA	Stemlite Model C-3 Lamp	ca. 1965	A Taste of Armageddon	52	
FOLLIS, JOHN	Architectural Pottery	USA	Ceramic Planter CP-21	1960s	The Man Trap	37	
GREENE, TOM	Feldman Lighting Company	USA	Torch-cut Brutalist Hanging Lamp	ca. 1960	A Taste of Armageddon	49	
HOGLUND, ERIK	Boda	Sweden	Tall-necked Bottle	1960s	A Taste of Armageddon	54	

DESIGNER	MANUFACTURER	COUNTRY OF ORIGIN	ITEM	ERA	EPISODE(S)	PAGE
JERÉ, CURTIS	Artisan House	USA	Snail and Foliage Brass Sculpture	1966	The Conscience of the King	42
JERÉ, CURTIS	Artisan House	USA	Raindrops Wall Mirror	1968	The *Enterprise* Incident	121
KAGAN, VLADIMIR-INSPIRED	Chromcraft	USA	Sculpta or "Unicorn" Chair	1966	The Trouble with Tribbles, Spock's Brain	87
KATAVOLOS, WILLIAM	Laverne	USA	T-chair	1952	Metamorphosis	79
KRESS, GEORGE	Royal McBee Corp.	USA	Royal Emperor Electric Typewriter	ca. 1965	Assignment: Earth	95

DESIGNER	MANUFACTURER	COUNTRY OF ORIGIN	ITEM	ERA	EPISODE(S)	PAGE	
LELAND, MALCOLM	Architectural Pottery	USA	Ceramic Candle Lantern	ca. 1951	The Corbomite Maneuver, Operation -- Annihilate!	33	
MCCOBB, PAUL	St. John Seating Corp.	USA	Origami Chair	1960	The Trouble with Tribbles	85	
MEADMORE, CLEMENT	Leif Wessman Associates	USA	Model 248 Sling Chair	1963	Metamorphosis	81	
MULHAUSER, GEORGE	Plycraft Inc.	USA	Mr. Chair	1960s	Assignment: Earth	92	
OBERHEIM, ROBERT	Braun AG	Germany	Nizo Super 8mm Cine Film Camera	1965	Patterns of Force	99	

DESIGNER	MANUFACTURER	COUNTRY OF ORIGIN	ITEM	ERA	EPISODE(S)	PAGE	
PAULIN, PIERRE	Artifort	France, Netherlands	Ribbon Chair	1965	The Cloud Minders	127	
PEABODY, LAWRENCE	Selig	USA	"Holiday" Series Lounge Chair Model 576	1960s	Operation -- Annihilate!	58	
PEPPER, ARTHUR	unknown	USA	Brutalist Ring	1960s	The *Enterprise* Incident	120	
PLATNER, WARREN	Knoll Inc.	USA	"Platner Collection" Chairs and Coffee Table	1966	A Taste of Armageddon	51	
RASMUSSEN, JORGEN AND MOLLER, ERIK	Kevi	Denmark	Swivel Chair Model KE3-1	1960s	A Taste of Armageddon	53	

DESIGNER	MANUFACTURER	COUNTRY OF ORIGIN	ITEM	ERA	EPISODE(S)	PAGE	
SAARINEN, EERO (ORIGINAL DESIGNER OF TULIP FURNITURE)	Knoll	USA	Pedestal or "Tulip" Furniture	1956	All episodes explored in this text	18	
STELLAN HØM, NIELS AND MEDELAIRE, CARTON	Stelton	Denmark	Chrome and Teak Salt and Pepper Shakers	1960s	Various episodes	103	
UMANOFF, ARTHUR	Madison Furniture Company	USA	Dimension 2400 Lounge Chair (modified for Captain's command chair)	1962	All episodes	20	
WAGENFELD, WILHELM	Württem-bergische Metallwaren-fabrik	Germany	Salt and Pepper Shakers	1952	The Man Trap	35	
VARIOUS	Empoli Glass	Italy	Colored Glassware	1960s	For the World is Hollow and I have Touched the Sky, The Tholian Web	123	

DESIGNER	MANUFACTURER	COUNTRY OF ORIGIN	ITEM	ERA	EPISODE(S)	PAGE	
VARIOUS (MCALLISTER TOM, GOODMAN DAVE, BERTOIA HARRY)	Various	USA	Spray Sculpture	1966	The Cloud Minders	129	
UNKNOWN	Rya	Denmark, Finland, Norway, Sweden	Shag Rug	1960s	For the World is Hollow and I have Touched the Sky	124	
UNKNOWN	Murano	Italy	Glass Bowl	1950s	The Tholian Web	109	
UNKNOWN	RS Associates LTD	Canada	Expo '67 Side Tables	1967	Assignment: Earth	90	
UNKNOWN	General Fireproofing Co.	USA	Aluminum Chair Model 2123	1932	Assignment: Earth	94	

DESIGNER	MANUFACTURER	COUNTRY OF ORIGIN	ITEM	ERA	EPISODE(S)	PAGE	
UNKNOWN	Prescolite	USA	Hanging Pendant Light	1960s	Court Martial	45	
UNKNOWN	George Dickel Brewery	USA	Saurian Brandy Decanter	1960s	Various episodes	100	
UNKNOWN	Shure Brothers Inc.	USA	Unidyne and Unisphere Microphones	1960s	Various episodes	107	
UNKNOWN	Aluminum Company of America (Alcoa)	USA	Alshade™ Decorative Aluminum Screens	1960s	Various episodes	104	

RIGHT Matt Jefferies' sketch for the never-built set of the personal quarters of Natira, High Priestess of Yonada. From "For the World is Hollow and I have Touched the Sky."

NATIRA'S QTRS.
065

INDEX

A

Additional Living System, 119
Albert C. Martin and Associates, 56
Alcoa Alshade® Screen, 104
Alshade Decorative Aluminum Screens, 160
"Alternative Factor" episode, 105
Aluminum Chair Model 2123, 159
Aluminum Company of America (Alcoa), 104, 160
"Amok Time" episode, 109
Architectural Pottery, 50
    Ceramic Candle Lantern, 156
    Ceramic Planter CP-21, 154
    ceramic planters, 10, 37
    Modular Standing Lantern, 32–33
    Stoneware Ceramic Vessel, 153
art directors, 23. See also Jefferies, Matt
Artifort, 157
Artisan House
    Raindrops Wall Mirror, 121, 155
    Snail & Foliage brass sculpture, 155
artists, 75
"Assignment: Earth" episode, 88–95, 152
    Aluminum Chair Model 2123, 159
    Boomerang Executive T-series desk, 90, 153
    Expo '67 side tables, 90, 159
    Goodform adjustable aluminum chair model #2123, 94
    Hollywood Regency Tufted Bucket Swivel Chairs and Couch, 91
    Mr. Chair, 92–93, 156
    Royal Emperor Electric Typewriter, 94–95, 155
Aztec god, 110

B

Barton, Arthur, 63
Baughman, Milo, 41, 153
Bauhaus movement, 12
Becket, Welton D., 65
Bertoia, Harry
    Brutalism style, 135
    Spray sculpture, 129, 159
Béton Brut, 132
Biddiscombe, Carl, 55, 154

Boda, 54, 155
Boomerang Executive T-series desk, 90, 153
Borsani, Osvaldo, 90, 153
bottles, 54–55, 154
Bowie, William, 133, 135
Braun AG, 156
The Bridge, USS *Enterprise*, 14–23
    Burke chair use on, 17–19
    Captain's command chair on, 20–21
    Matt Jefferies designer of, 16
Bronze figurative sculpture, 138
Brooks, Rolland M., 23
Brutalism, 73, 130–141
    architecture, 132–133, 139
    Brutalist Ring, 120, 157
    Brutalist table base, 134
    sculptures, 134–135, 137, 140
budget for *Star Trek*, 13
Burke, Maurice, 17–19, 151
Burke chair, 17–19, 29
Burke Inc., 153

C

cabins
    of Captain Kirk, 46, 110
    metal cabin, 80
    of Mr. Spock's, 109
    of Uhura's, 109
    on USS *Enterprise*, 108
    of Yeoman Janice Rand, 110
    of Zefram Cochrane, 66
"The Cage" episode, 18, 20, 26–29
    matte painting in, 68, 70
    women fashion in, 112
cameras, 156
Captain Kirk
    quarters in "Court Martial," 46
    quarters in "Obsession," 110
Captain's command chair, 20–21
Cardin, Pierre, 113
Ceramic Candle Lantern, 156
ceramic figures, 108
    Aztec god, 110
    Stoneware Ceramic Vessel, 153
Ceramic Planter CP-21, 154
chairs
    ads for, 147–148, 151
    Aluminum Chair Model 2123, 159
    Burke chair, 17–19, 29
    Captain's command chair, 20–21

Dimension 2400 Lounge Chair, 158
Elda Chair, 119, 153
Goodform adjustable aluminum chair model #2123, 94
high back lounge chair, 58–59
"Holiday" Series Lounge Chair Model 576, 157
Hollywood Regency Tufted Bucket Swivel Chairs and Couch, 92–93
KE3-1 swivel chair, 53
Model 3 T-Chair, 79
Model 248 Sling Chair, 81, 156
Mr. Chair, 92–93, 149
Origami chair, 11, 85–86, 156
Platner Collection, 155
Ribbon chair, 127–128, 140, 155
Sculpta chair, 87, 153
Swivel Chair, 27, 46
Swivel Chair Model KE3-1, 157
Swivel Rocker chair, 41
in "A Taste of Armageddon" episode, 51
    T-Chair, 153
    Tulip chair, 17–19, 153, 158
    Unicorn chair, 87
Chromcraft, 87, 155
Chrome and Teak Salt and Pepper Shakers, 158
"The Cloud Minders" episode, 11, 126–129
    Brutalism in, 139, 140, 141
    matte painting in, 74
    Ribbon chair, 127–128, 157
    sketches of, 60–61, 141
    Spray sculpture, 129
    storyboard for, 72, 74
Cochrane, Zefram, 140
coffee tables. See tables
Colombo, Joe, 121, 153
Colored Glassware, 158
Columnlite Models 'G' & 'C-4', 39–40, 154
Comfort, 153
"The Conscience of the King" episode, 38–43
    Brutalism in, 136
    Columnlite Models 'G' & 'C-4', 39–40, 154
    matte painting in, 70
    Saurian brandy decanter, 100
    Snail & Foliage brass sculpture,

42–43, 155
    Swivel Rocker chair, 41, 153
"The Corbomite Maneuver" episode, 10, 30–33
    Ceramic Candle Lantern, 156
    women fashion in, 112
Corbusier, Le, 132
"Cosmocorps" clothing line, 113
couches, 46
    ads for, 147
    Hollywood Regency Tufted Bucket Swivel Chairs and Couch, 91
"Court Martial" episode, 44–47
    decorative grills in, 105
    Hanging Pendant Light, 45, 160
    in Kirk's quarters, 46
    matte painting in, 70
    microphone used in, 107
    tables in, 47
CP-21, 37
Cressey, David, 50, 153
Curry, William
    Columnlite Models 'G' & 'C-4', 39–40, 152
    Stemlite Model C-3 Lamp, 52, 154
Curry lamp, 52

D

"Dagger of the Mind" episode, 70
D'Angelo, Floyd, 67
Danish Modern salt and pepper shakers, 103
D'Angelo House, 67
decanters
    George Dickel whisky decanter, 101
    Saurian Brandy Decanter, 100, 160
decorative grills, 104–105. See also screens
    Alshade Decorative Aluminum Screens, 160
    in "Court Martial" episode, 105
Design Line, Inc., 39–40, 52
    Columnlite Models 'G' & 'C-4', 154
    Stemlite Model C-3 Lamp, 154
Desilu's Culver City Studio, 20
desks, 90, 153
"Devil in the Dark" episode, 62
Dimension 2400 Lounge Chair, 158
Draper, Dorothy, 89, 91
Dwyer, John

Brutalism, 136
  interview with, 10–11
  set decorators, 83

E

El Matador ad, 145
"Elaan of Troyius" episode, 9–10
Elda Chair, 119, 151
"The Empath" episode, 141
Emperor Electric Typewriter, 94–95
Empoli Glass, 123, 158
"Enemy Within" episode, 100, 110
"The *Enterprise* Incident" episode,
  118–121
  Brutalism in, 136
  Brutalist Ring, 120, 157
  Elda Chair, 119, 151
  Raindrops Wall Mirror, 121, 153
episodes
  "Assignment: Earth," 94–95
  Alshade Decorative Aluminum
    Screens, 160
  "Alternative Factor," 105
  "Amok Time," 109
  "Assignment: Earth," 88–95, 150
    Boomerang Executive desk, 90
    Boomerang Executive T-series
    desk, 151
    Expo '67 side tables, 90, 159
    Goodform adjustable aluminum
    chair model #2123, 94
    Hollywood Regency Tufted
    Bucket Swivel Chairs and
    Couch, 91
    Mr. Chair, 92–93, 156
    Royal Emperor Electric
    Typewriter, 155
  "The Cage," 18, 26–29
    matte painting in, 68, 70
    women fashion in, 112
    Chrome and Teak Salt and
    Pepper Shakers, 156
  "The Cloud Minders," 11, 126–129
    Brutalism in, 142, 143
    matte painting in, 74
    Ribbon chair, 127–128, 157
    sketches of, 60–61, 143
    Spray sculpture, 129, 159
    storyboard for, 72, 74
  "The Conscience of the King,"
    38–43
    Brutalism in, 136

Columnlite Models 'G' & 'C-4',
  39–40, 154
  matte painting in, 70
  Saurian brandy decanter, 100
  Snail & Foliage brass sculpture,
  42–43, 155
  Swivel Rocker chair, 41, 152
"The Corbomite Maneuver," 10,
  30–33
  Ceramic Candle Lantern, 156
  women fashion in, 112
"Court Martial," 44–47
  decorative grills in, 105
  Hanging Pendant Light, 45, 160
  Kirk's quarters in, 46
  matte painting in, 70
  microphone used in, 107
  tables in, 47, 50
"Dagger of the Mind," 70
"Devil in the Dark," 62
  Dimension 2400 Lounge Chair,
  158
"Elaan of Troyius," 9–10
"The Empath," 139
"Enemy Within," 98, 110
"The *Enterprise* Incident," 118–121
  Brutalism in, 136
  Brutalist Ring, 120, 157
  Elda Chair, 119, 151
  Raindrops Wall Mirror, 121, 155
"Errand of Mercy," 68
"Journey to Babel," 102
"The Man Trap," 10, 34–37
  Ceramic Planter CP-21, 154
  Salt & Pepper Shakers, 158
"Metamorphosis," 66, 78–82, 152
  Brutalism in, 138
  metal cabin, 80
  Model 3 T-Chair, 79
  Model 248 Chair, 81, 156
  string art, 82
  T-Chair, 155
"Obsession," 108, 110
"Operation -- Annihilate!" 56–59,
  63–65
  Brutalism in, 138
  high back lounge chair, 56–59
"Holiday" Series Lounge Chair
  Model 576, 157
  Modular Standing Lantern,
  32–33
"Patterns of Force," 99
  Nizo Super 8 Cine Film camera,

156
  Super 8MM movie camera, 99
  Pedestal Furniture, 151, 156
"Requiem for Methuselah"
  Brutalism in, 139
  matte painting in, 68–69
"Return to Tomorrow," 102–103
  Saurian Brandy Decanter, 160
"Spock's Brain," 106
  Spray sculpture, 159
"A Taste of Armageddon," 11,
  48–55
  Brutalism in, 136–137, 138
  chairs and coffee table, 51
  Hanging Lamp, 49
  KE3-1 swivel chair, 53
  matte painting in, 71
"Platner Collection" Chairs and
  Coffee Table, 157
  Stemlite Model C-3 lamp, 52,
  154
  Stoneware Ceramic Vessel, 50,
  153
  Swivel Chair Model KE3-1, 157
  tall bottle, 54–55
  Tall-necked Bottle, 154
  Torch-cut Brutalist Hanging
  Lamp, 154
"The Tholian Web"
  Glass Bowl, 159
  Uhura's cabin, 109
"Tomorrow is Yesterday," 17–19
"The Trouble with Tribbles," 11,
  84–87
  Origami chair, 85–86, 156
  Sculpta chair, 87, 155
  Unisphere microphones, 160
"The Way to Eden," 22
"Where No Man Has Gone Before,"
  18
  matte painting in, 70
  women fashion in, 112
"Whom Gods Destroy," 18
"Wink of an Eye," 95, 130–131, 141
"For the World is Hollow and I
  Have Touched the Sky," 109,
  122–125
  Colored Glassware, 156
  decorative grills in, 106
  Empoli Glass, 123
  Rya rug, 124–125
  Shag Rug, 159
"Errand of Mercy" episode, 68

Evans, Paul, 133, 134
Expo '67 side tables, 90, 159

F

fashion, 112–113
Feinberg, Irving, 115, 121
Feldman Lighting Company, 49, 152
Follis, John, 10, 37, 154
"For the World is Hollow and I Have
  Touched the Sky" episode, 109,
  122–125
  Colored Glassware, 158
  decorative grills in, 106
  Empoli Glass, 123
  Rya rug, 124–125
  Shag Rug, 159
Franz Joseph Designs, 107
Fromhold, Hal, 108, 110
futurist architecture, 60–75
  "Devil in the Dark" episode, 62
  on location shooting for, 62
  matte painting used for, 62, 68–75
  in "Metamorphosis" episode, 66
  Metropolis film, 67
  Zefram Cochrane's cabin, 66

G

Gary Seven's office, 95
General Fireproofing Company, 94
George Dickel Brewery, 160
George Dickel whisky decanter, 101
General Fireproofing Co., 159
Gerrold, David, 85–86
glassware
  Colored Glassware, 159
  Glass Bowl, 159
gold figurative sculpture, 137
Goodform adjustable aluminum
  chair model #2123, 94
Goodman, Dave, 129, 159
Greene, Tom
  Brutalism, 138
  Hanging Lamp, 49
  Torch-cut Brutalist Hanging Lamp,
  154
Gurian, Gerald, 141

H

Hanging Lamp, 49, 138
Hanging Pendant Light, 45, 159, 160

INDEX

hexagonal grille-work, 105
high back lounge chair, 56–59
Hoglund, Erik
    tall bottle, 54–55
    Tall-necked Bottle, 154
"Holiday" Series Lounge Chair Model
    576, 157
Hollywood Regency Tufted Bucket
    Swivel Chairs and Couch, 91

I

Ihlenfeld, Klaus, 133, 135

J

Jefferies, Matt, 16, 18–19, 66, 68
    Brutalism style, 143
    Captain's command chair design
        of, 20
    career of, 23
    design of briefing room table, 19
    design of the Bridge, 14–15
    drawing of Gary Seven's office, 95
    drawing of living quarters, 108
    drawings of Cloud City of Stratos,
        72, 74
    drawings of Gary Seven's office,
        95
    drawings of modernist cabin, 66
    drawings of steel panel cabin, 66
    drawings of torture chamber,
        74–75
    sketches of "Elaan of Troyius,"
        9–10
    sketches of "Errand of Mercy," 68
    sketches of "The Cloud Minders"
        episode, 60–61, 141
    sketches of "Wink of an Eye," 95,
        130–131
    storyboard for "The Cloud
        Minders," 72, 74
Jere, Curtis
    Brutalism, 135, 136, 137
    Raindrops Wall Mirror, 155
    Snail & Foliage brass sculpture,
        42–43, 153
jewelry, 120
Joseph, Franz, 102, 107
"Journey to Babel" episode, 102

K

K-7 lounge scene, 85–86
Kagan, Vladimir, 155
Katavolos, William
    Model 3 T-Chair, 79
    T-Chair, 153
KE3-1 swivel chair, 53
Kelley, Douglas, 79
Kepenyes, Pal, 120
Kevi, 155
Kirk. See Captain Kirk
Knoll Company, 18
Knoll Inc., 51
    Pedestal Furniture, 158
    "Platner Collection" Chairs and
        Coffee Table, 157
Kress, George, 155

L

lamps
    Hanging Lamp, 49
    Hanging Pendant Light, 160
    Stemlite Model C-3 Lamp, 52, 154
    Torch-cut Brutalist Hanging Lamp,
        154
lanterns
    Ceramic Candle Lantern, 156
    Modular Standing Lantern, 32–33
Lasdun, Denys, 132
Laverne, 79, 155
Leif Wessman Associates INC, 81,
    156
Leland, Malcolm, 32–33
lights, 45. See also lamps; lanterns
"Lily pads" coffee table, 135
Littell, Ross, 79
living quarters, on USS Enterprise,
    108
lounge chairs, 58–59

M

Madison Furniture Company, 20,
    32–33, 158
Malcolm, Leland, 156
"The Man Trap" episode, 10, 34–37
    Ceramic Planter CP-21, 154
    Salt & Pepper Shakers, 158
March, Marvin, 55, 152
matte painting

in "The Cage" episode, 68, 70
in "The Cloud Minders" episode,
    74
in "The Conscience of the King"
    episode, 70
in "Court Martial" episode, 70
futurist architecture, 62, 68–75
in "Requiem for Methuselah"
    episode, 68–69
in "A Taste of Armageddon"
    episode, 71
in "Where No Man Has Gone
    Before" episode, 70
McCallister, Tom, 129, 159
McCobb, Paul, 11, 85–86, 156
Meadmore, Clement, 81, 156
metal cabin, 80
"Metamorphosis" episode, 66,
    78–82, 152
    Brutalism in, 138
    metal cabin, 80
    Model 3 T-Chair, 79
    Model 248 Sling Chair, 81, 156
    string art, 82
    T-Chair, 155
Metropolis film, 67
microphones, 107, 160
midcentury advertising, 144–151
Midcentury Modern Design, 12–13
Midcentury Modern furniture, 10
mirrors, 155
Model 3 T-Chair, 79
Model 248 Sling Chair, 81, 156
Modern Baroque style, 91
Modernism, 12
Modular Standing Lantern, 32–33
Moller, Erik, 53, 157
Mr. Chair, 92–93, 147, 156
Mr. Spock's cabin, 109
Mulhauser, George, 92–93, 156
Murano, 109, 159
Museum of Pop Culture, 20

N

Nizo Super 8 Cine Film camera, 99,
    156
Notre-Dame du Hait Chapel, 132

O

Oberheim, Robert, 99, 156
"Obsession" episode, 108, 110

"Operation -- Annihilate!" episode,
    56–59
    Brutalism, 139
    futurist architecture of, 63–65
    high back lounge chair, 56–59
    "Holiday" Series Lounge Chair
        Model 576, 157
    Modular Standing Lantern, 32–33
Origami chair, 11, 87, 156

P

"Patterns of Force" episode, 99
    Nizo Super 8 Cine Film camera,
        156
    Super 8MM movie camera, 99
Paulin, Pierre
    Brutalism style, 140
    Ribbon chair, 127–128, 157
Peabody, Lawrence, 58
    high back lounge chair, 58
    "Holiday" Series Lounge Chair
        Model 576, 157
Pedestal Furniture, 153, 158
"pencil cactus," 42
Pepper, Arthur, 120, 157
planters
    Architectural Pottery planter, 10
    ceramic, 37, 154
Platner, Warren, 51, 157
Platner Collection, 11, 51
Plycraft INC., 92–93, 154
Pollack, Reginald, 114–115
Prescolite, 45, 160
primitivism, 109–110
Product Line Ltd., 20
prop man, 10–11

R

Raindrops Wall Mirror, 121, 155
Rand, Yeoman Janice, 112
Rasmussen, Jorgen, 53, 157
raw concrete, 132
Regency Moderne, 91
"Requiem for Methuselah" episode
    Brutalism in, 139
    matte painting in, 68–69
"Return to Tomorrow" episode,
    102–103
Ribbon chair, 127–128, 142, 157
Richards furniture store, 11
Robin Hood Gardens, 133

Roddenberry, Gene, 29, 33, 94–95
room dividers, 104–105
Royal Electress typewriter, 95
Royal Emperor Electric Typewriter, 155
Royal McBee Corp., 155
Royal National Theater, 132
RS Associates LTD, 90, 159
Rudolph, Paul, 133
rugs
    Rya rug, 124–125
    Shag Rug, 159

S

Saarinen, Eero, 17–19, 158
Salt & Pepper Shakers, 35–36, 102–103, 158
Sam Kirk's laboratory, 65
Saurian Brandy Decanter, 100, 160
Schoenberg Hall, 65
screens, 160
Sculpta chair, 87, 155
sculptures
    Bronze figurative sculpture, 139
    Brutalism style, 134–135, 137, 140
    gold figurative sculpture, 138
    Snail & Foliage brass sculpture, 42–43, 153
    Spray sculpture, 129, 159
Seandel, Silas
    Brutalism style, 133
    wall sculpture, 134, 138
Season One, 24–59
    "The Cage" episode, 26–29
    "The Conscience of the King" episode, 38–43, 136
    "The Corbomite Maneuver" episode, 30–33
    "Court Martial" episode, 44–47
    "The Man Trap" episode, 34–37
    "Operation -- Annihilate!" episode, 56–59
    "A Taste of Armageddon" episode, 48–55
Season Two, 76–95
    "Assignment: Earth" episode, 88–95
    "Metamorphosis" episode, 78–82
    "Patterns of Force" episode, 99
    "The Trouble with Tribbles" episodes, 84–87
Season Three, 116–129

T

tables
    Brutalist table base, 134
    coffee tables, 51, 135
    in "Court Martial" episode, 47, 50
    design of briefing room table, 19
    Expo '67 side tables, 90, 159
    "Lily pads" coffee table, 135
    in "A Taste of Armageddon" episode, 51

"The Cloud Minders" episode, 126–129, 142, 143
"The *Enterprise* Incident" episode, 118–121, 136
Selig, 157
set decorators
    Biddiscombe, Carl, 55, 150
    Dwyer, John, 83
    Feinberg, Irving, 121
    Stone, Joseph, 125
set designers, 23
Shag Rug, 159
Shure Brothers Inc., 160
Shure Microphone, 107
side tables. *See* tables
Smithson, Alison & Peter, 133
Snail & Foliage brass sculpture, 42–43, 153
sofas. *See* couches
Sonambient sculpture, 135
Space Park, 63–65
"Spock's Brain" episode, 106
Spray sculpture, 129, 159
St. John Seating Corp, 85, 156
Star Trek Star Fleet Technical Manual (Joseph), 102, 107
Stellan, Hom, 103, 158
Stelton shaker, 103
Stemlite Model C-3 Lamp, 52, 154
Stone, Edward Durell, 104
Stone, Joseph, 125
Stoneware Ceramic Vessel, 50, 153
store ads, 142–149
storyboards, 68, 72
string art, 82
Sturm, Craig, 63
Super 8MM movie camera, 99
surgical scalpels, 102
Swivel Chair, 27
Swivel Chair Model KE3-1, 53, 157
Swivel Rocker Club chair, 41, 153

tall bottle, 54–55
Tall-necked Bottle, 154
"A Taste of Armageddon" episode, 48–55
    Brutalism in, 137–138, 140
    KE3-1 swivel chair, 53
    matte painting in, 71
    Origami chair, 11
    "Platner Collection" Chairs and Coffee Table, 51, 157
    Stemlite Model C-3 Lamp, 52, 154
    Stoneware Ceramic Vessel, 50, 153
    Swivel Chair Model KE3-1, 157
    Tall-necked Bottle, 54–55, 154
    Torch-cut Brutalist Hanging Lamp, 49, 154
T-Chair, 79, 155
Tecno, 90, 153
Thayer Coggin, 153
"The Tholian Web" episode
    Glass Bowl, 159
    Uhura's cabin, 109
    "the tire," 37
Tom Greene Brutalist torch-cut lamp, 49
"Tomorrow is Yesterday" episode, 13
Torch-cut Brutalist Hanging Lamp, 154
torch-cut lamps, 49, 54
"The Trouble with Tribbles" episode, 11, 84–87
    Origami chair, 85–86, 156
    Sculpta chair, 87, 155
TRW Defense and Space Campus, 63–65
Tulip chair, 17–19
Tulip Furniture, 153, 158
typewriters
    Emperor Electric Typewriter, 94–95
    Royal Emperor Electric Typewriter, 155

U

Uhura's cabin, 109
Umanoff, Arthur, 20–21
    Dimension 2400 Lounge Chair, 158
    Swivel Chair, 27
Unicorn chair, 87, 155
Unisphere microphones, 160
Unité d' Habitation, 132

USS Enterprise
    the Bridge on, 14–23
        Burke chair use on, 17–19
        Captain's command chair on, 20–21
        Matt Jefferies designer of, 16
    cabins
        metal cabin, 80
        Mr. Spock's cabin, 109
        Uhura's cabin, 109
        on *USS Enterprise*, 108
        Yeoman Janice Rand's cabin, 110
        Zefram Cochrane's cabin, 66
    living quarters on, 108

V

Various, 159

W

Wagenfeld, Wilhelm, 35–36, 158
wall furniture ad, 147–148, 151
wall mirror, 121
wall sculpture, 134, 142
"The Way to Eden" episode, 22
"Where No Man Has Gone Before" episode, 18
    matte painting in, 70
    women fashion in, 112
Whitlock, Albert, 68–70, 75
Whitney, Grace Lee, 112
"Whom Gods Destroy" episode, 18
Will, Philip, 104
"Wink of an Eye" episode, 95, 130–131
Wotruba, Fritz, 132
Wotruba Church, 132
Württembergische Metallwarenfabrik, 35–36, 158

Y

Yale School of Architecture, 133
Yeoman Janice Rand's cabin, 110

Z

Zefram Cochrane's cabin, 66

CREDITS

Cover concept by Gary Wexler.

All images were provided courtesy of the **Star Trek Archive & Library**, **ViacomCBS**, with the exception of the following:

123RF: 133 (Rudolph Hall; ref. 21714248)

1967 Montreal Expo: 90 (postcard)

Alamy: 132-133 (Brutalist architecture; refs. DCY6JP, E1GEMK, JJ1YB2, R00K92, EPYMN4)

Aluminum Company of America: 104-105

Alternative Furnishings, Inc.: 135 (Ihlenfeld table base)

Annex Marketplace: 41 (photo by Danielle Quiroz)

Architectural Pottery Catalog 1964: 37 (Follis planters ad), 50 (Cressey ad)

Archive Pierre Cardin: 113 (Yoshi Takata photos)

Artifort: 128 (ad)

Artract: 55 (Kevi chair)

ArtResource/MoMA: 35, 81

Oliver Brown: 79 (T chair)

Balder Design: 55 (Hoglund bottle)

Barbarella Home: 27

Braun AG: 99 (camera ad)

Connors Roth Art & Design: 20

Bill Cotter: 7 (Doug Drexler photo)

Bill Curry Design Line Archives and Form Portfolios: 39 (photo by Glenn Dodge), 40 (photo by Bill Curry), 52

Chromcraft Inc: 87 (1966 ad)

Classic-Modern.co.uk: 53, 124

Converso: 49, 76

Cosmo Art & Design: 134 (Evans sculpture)

Dan Chavkin: 67 (D'Angelo house), 101 (Dickel decanter), 103, 108 (Fromhold sculpture),

Design Finmark: 125

Anita Doohan Dwyer: 83 (Dwyer photo)

Empoli: 123 (ad)

Farmer Auctions: 109

Furnish Me Vintage: 87

Galere W. Palm Beach: 134 (Seandel sculpture)

George Dickel Brewery: 101 (ad)

Gerald Gurian: 8, 14, 19, 21, 23, 29, 36 (Jeanne Bal photo), 60, 66 (Jefferies drawings), 68, 69, 71 (set still, matte painting), 72, 74, 75, 83 (Dwyer on-set photo), 95 (storyboard), 96, 108 (Jefferies sketch), 112 (publicity still), 130, 143, 161

Getty Images: 36, 128 (Pierre Paulin photo)

Dex Hamilton/Automaton Modern: 134 (Evans table base)

Harvey's on Beverly: 94

Gary Hutzel: 7 (1964-65 Expo photos)

Independent magazine, October 1961: 86 (Henry's ad)

J. Paul Getty Trust, Getty Research Institute, Los Angeles. (2004.R. 10): 63 (photo by Julius Shulman)

Knoll, Inc.: 11 (Platner furniture ad), 17 (Tulip chairs)

Laurence Peabody Designs: 58 (ad)

Le Shoppe Too: 134 (anonymous sculpture)

Link Auction Gallery: 42

Los Angeles Modern Auctions: 4 (Warren Platner chairs), 32, 37 (Follis planters), 50 (Cressey ceramic vessel)

Los Angeles Times (Home magazine): 144, 147-151

Midcentury Sacramento: 90 (octagonal table)

Naked Modernism: 51 (Platner table)

Pamono: 18, 109 (Murano bowl)

AUTHOR BIOS

Penguin Random House: 102, 107 (artwork ©1975 by Franz Joseph Designs and used with permission)

Prescolite: 45

Royal McBee Company: 95 (ad)

St. John Seating Co.:: 11 (McCobb chair ad)

Sgustok Design: 99 (Braun camera)

Shure Brothers: 107 (mic ad)

Solo Modern: 129

Smithsonian American Art Museum (Gift of Container Corporation of America 1984. 124.239): 115

Star Trek **Archive & Library:** 112 (publicity still)

STM Furniture Forum: 20 (Madison furniture ad)

Style House: 93

The Swanky Abode: 24, 58 (Peabody chair)

Eric Thevenot/Blend Interiors: 137 (Greene lamp)

TrekCore.com/Gene Roddenberry Archives: 66 (Jefferies sketch)

UCLA Library Archives: 65

Universum Film A Studios: 67 (*Metropolis* still)

Venfield NYC: 137 (bronze sculpture)

Vintage in Bloom: 120

Wright Auction: 4 (Eero Saarinen chairs), 5 (Pierre Paulin chairs, Paul McCobb Origami chairs), 17 (Tulip chairs), 51 (Platner chair), 79 (T chair), 86 (Origami chairs), 90 (Borsani desk), 121, 127

Max Zarri Casa d'Aste Della Roca: 92

Zorrobot.de: 116, 119

Zus Korsten Haarlem Netherlands: 123 (Empoli vases)

DAN CHAVKIN began his photographic career in 1992, studying at the prestigious school Art Center College of Design in Pasadena, California. Upon graduating, he moved to New York City to work as a professional photographer, shooting celebrity portraiture for various top magazines. An avid aficionado of all things modernist, Dan began collecting midcentury modern furniture, and vintage film posters, book covers, and periodicals as a way of feeding his passion for modernism. Returning to Los Angeles, his photographic work consisted of human-interest stories for numerous national publications and advertising campaigns.

In the summer of 2008, upon a trip to Palm Springs, Dan discovered the wealth of midcentury modern architecture in the same desert city he had often visited as a child. Inspired by the architecture and its relation to the landscape, he began photographing the many examples of midcentury modern architecture in Palm Springs and throughout Coachella Valley.

Since then, Dan has received critical acclaim for his architectural work from numerous modern preservation organizations, magazine publications, and modernist homeowners alike.

In 2014, he co-authored a book on the husband-and-wife midcentury modern designers Jerome and Evelyn Ackerman, titled *Hand-In-Hand*, and in 2016, Dan published *Unseen Midcentury Desert Modern,* a photographic survey of hidden, often overlooked, desert modern residences, buildings, and houses of worship throughout the Coachella Valley.

Dan lives and works in Palm Springs, California.

BRIAN MCGUIRE earned both his undergraduate degree in Molecular Biology and doctorate in Biochemistry from Vanderbilt University. During his career in new drug development, he generated numerous publications and abstracts for technical journals. In 2006 he acquired one of the all-steel houses designed by Donald Wexler in Palm Springs, where he became active in several preservation organizations. Through this, he developed an amateur appreciation for midcentury architecture and design. In 2012, he successfully got his Wexler-designed house listed in the National Register of Historic Places, engaging photographer Dan Chavkin for the application. McGuire currently lives in the Santa Rosa Valley area of Ventura County, California, and is also a part-time resident of Kansas City, where he grew up an avid *Star Trek* fan.

weldon**owen**

CEO Raoul Goff
VP PUBLISHER, WELDON OWEN Roger Shaw
ASSOCIATE PUBLISHER Mariah Bear
EDITORIAL DIRECTOR Katie Killebrew
VP CREATIVE Chrissy Kwasnik
VP MANUFACTURING Alix Nicholaeff
ART DIRECTOR Allister Fein
EDITOR Ian Cannon
SENIOR PRODUCTION MANAGER Greg Steffen

Weldon Owen would also like to thank Mark Nichol for his editorial expertise, and Kevin Broccoli of BIM for the index.

AUTHOR ACKNOWLEDGMENTS

First of all, the authors want to thank Risa Kessler at ViacomCBS, without whom this book would not be possible. It was Risa who believed in the project and enthusiastically took it to market. We are forever grateful for her hard work and dedication.

To our very dedicated publisher Mariah Bear and editor Ian Cannon at Weldon Owen of Insight Editions, we extend our appreciation for all of their tenacity, perseverance, insight, and guidance.

Art Director Allister Fein deserves special praise for his design and layout of the book. He did such an incredible job realizing our vision with his creativity, problem-solving, and rapid turnaround. We thank him for his unwavering commitment.

We thank designer Gary Wexler for his superb cover design. He proves that you can judge a book by its cover. Also, we thank him for giving us access to his Hal Fromhold sculpture.

We are indebted to Marian Cordry, Director of the *Star Trek* Archive and Library of ViacomCBS, who tirelessly retrieved all of the episode images and additionally gave us access to behind-the-scenes shots and publicity stills seldom if ever seen by the public. We thank Marian for her irreplaceable contribution to the book.

We also wish to extend special thanks to Gerald Gurian who, on so many levels, propelled this project forward. He generously gave us access to his extensive private *Star Trek* collection including the sketches of Matt Jefferies and numerous production stills—not to mention his own recollection and knowledge of the story of Star Trek. His responsiveness was awesome, usually replying on the very day of our request. Gerald's own series of books: *To Boldly Go: Rare Photos from the TOS Soundstage*, were an invaluable source of both information and inspiration. Because of individuals like Gerald Gurian, the *Star Trek* legend lives on.

Many other individuals were instrumental in assisting us in the identification and research of objects of interest; these are, alphabetically, Steve Aldana, Katherine Alvarado of the University of California at Los Angeles, Patrick Barry of Bon Vivant, Anna Carnick of Pamono, Anthony Chong, Eric Curry, Brad Dunning, Alexandro Fabbroni, Thomas Guttandin, Dave Harker, Allison Jakobovic of Penguin Random House LLC, Allison Klein of Kraft Auctions, Ron and Barbara Marshall of Palm Springs Preservation Foundation, Courtney Newman of Modernway, Gerard O'Brien, Rod Parks of Retro Inferno, Julie Silliman, Ben Stork of Galerie XX, Todd Simeone of Wright Auctions, Bob Tauber of Prescolite, Julio Ventura of Ventura's, and Lissette Verhorst.